THEORIES OF
IN PERSOI
SOCIAL PSYCHOLOGY

An Enduring Problem in Psychology

SELECTED READINGS

Edited by

RICHARD C. TEEVAN
Bucknell University

AND

ROBERT C. BIRNEY
Amherst College

AN INSIGHT BOOK

D. VAN NOSTRAND COMPANY, INC.
PRINCETON, NEW JERSEY

TORONTO   LONDON

NEW YORK

D. VAN NOSTRAND COMPANY, INC.
120 Alexander St., Princeton, New Jersey
(*Principal Office*)
24 West 40 Street, New York 18, New York

D. VAN NOSTRAND COMPANY, LTD.
358, Kensington High Street, London, W.14, England

D. VAN NOSTRAND COMPANY (Canada), LTD.
25 Hollinger Road, Toronto 16, Canada

———————

COPYRIGHT © 1964, BY
D. VAN NOSTRAND COMPANY, INC.

———————

Published simultaneously in Canada by
D. VAN NOSTRAND COMPANY (Canada), LTD.

———————

PRINTED IN THE UNITED STATES OF AMERICA

Foreword
By the Editors of the Series

In the field of psychology we believe that the student ought to get the "feel" of experimentation by reading original source materials. In this way he can acquire a better understanding of the discipline by seeing scientific ideas grow and change. However, one of the main problems in teaching is the limited availability of these sources, which communicate most effectively the personality of the author and the excitement of ongoing research.

For these reasons we have decided to edit several books,* each devoted to a particular problem in psychology. In every case we attempt to select problems that have been and are controversial—that have been and still are alive. We intend to present these problems as a set of selected original articles, arranged in historical order and in order of progress in the field. We believe that it is important for the student to see that theories and researches build on what has gone before; that one study leads to another, that theory leads to research and then to revision of theory. We believe that *telling* the student this does not make the same kind of impression as letting him see it happen in actuality. The idea is for the student to read and build ideas for himself.

Suggestions for Use—These readings books can be used by the student in either of two ways. They are organized so that, with the help of the instructor (or of the students if used in seminars), a topic can be covered at length and in depth. This would necessitate lectures or discussions on articles not covered in the series to fill in the gaps. On the other hand, each book taken alone will give a student a good idea of the problem being covered and its historical background as well as its present state and the direction it seems to be taking.

---

* (Pub. note: a sub-series within the Insight Book Series.)

Contents

Introduction

Concepts of motivation have a way of appearing in nearly every model of behavior. Yet motivation itself is a topic area and courses are devoted to its study. Thus the teacher of such courses finds he must draw on a wide variety of behavior theories without being able to assume or teach an acquaintance in depth of these sources. This book and its companion, *Theories of Motivation in Learning*, contain selections taken from various system builders. The selections are chosen to reveal the manner in which motivational questions are subject to conception from rather disparate points of view.

Although Freud's theory of mind is so dynamically cast as to appear almost totally motivational in character, we have chosen his treatment of instincts as the most concise statement he made in reply to the question, "What is it that motivates man?" McDougall was similarly occupied, and the form which his answer takes differs quite markedly from Freud's. This statement is the one he wished to stand by, following the critical reaction to his earlier statement of human motivation published ten years before.

Turning to the issue of the manner in which motives affect the behavior of human beings, we begin with Allport's still classic statement of the substantive transformation of motives through their integration by experience. Murray presents the case for the attributes of the motivational constructs which set them apart, while McClelland and Clark trace the development of the motivational process through encounter with the environment. Such processes rest on the assumption of certain basic native capacities for reinforcement, and Maslow's return to Freud's question reveals the possibility of "instincts" which have been difficult to identify and appreciate as motivational components in personality.

The last two selections emphasize the motivational contribution made by the environment, and raise the possibility of accounting for motivational phenomena as derivatives of the interaction of other constructs not usually cast as motives. Festinger assumes that the ordering of cognitions about the world has a certain motivational character to it, shows how this sets in motion various behaviors in the social psychology of the individual as he encounters various opinions at variance with his own, and traces the processes of resolution which follow. Rotter also confronts us with the effects of experience, with situations as a key variable in permitting the prediction of behavior which we customarily call "motivated."

If these selections display any sort of order, it may be that they take the student from the inside to the outside, from the unaware to the totally cognized, from motivation conceived as a set of prime movers to motivation conceived as a set of derived behaviors. We leave further abstraction to the student and the teacher. We present this group as representing those strains of theory currently existing side by side in the effort to analyze motivation.

Lewisburg, Pa.   R.C.T.
Amherst, Mass.   R.C.B.

Instincts and Their Vicissitudes

SIGMUND FREUD

The view is often defended that sciences should be
built up on clear and sharply defined basal concepts. In
actual fact no science, not even the most exact, begins
with such definitions. The true beginning of scientific
activity consists rather in describing phenomena and
then in proceeding to group, classify and correlate them.
Even at the stage of description it is not possible to avoid
applying certain abstract ideas to the material in hand,
ideas derived from various sources and certainly not the
fruit of the new experience only. Still more indispensable
are such ideas—which will later become the basal concepts of the science—as the material is further elaborated.
They must at first necessarily possess some measure of
uncertainty; there can be no question of any clear delimi-
tation of their content. So long as they remain in this
condition, we come to an understanding about their
meaning by repeated references to the material of observation, from which we seem to have deduced our
abstract ideas, but which is in point of fact subject to
them. Thus, strictly speaking, they are in the nature of
conventions; although everything depends on their being
chosen in no arbitrary manner, but determined by the
important relations they have to the empirical material—
relations that we seem to divine before we can clearly
recognize and demonstrate them. It is only after more
searching investigation of the field in question that we
are able to formulate with increased clarity the scientific
concepts underlying it, and progressively so to modify

Excerpted from *The Collected Papers of Sigmund Freud*,
Vol. IV, 1949, Ernest Jones, Editor; Joan Riviere (trans.).
The Hogarth Press Ltd. with permission of the publishers.

these concepts that they become widely applicable and at the same time consistent logically. Then, indeed, it may be time to immure them in definitions. The progress of science, however, demands a certain elasticity even in these definitions. The science of physics furnishes an excellent illustration of the way in which even those 'basal concepts' that are firmly established in the form of definitions are constantly being altered in their content.

A conventional but still rather obscure basal concept of this kind, which is nevertheless indispensable to us in psychology, is that of an *instinct*. Let us try to ascertain what is comprised in this conception by approaching it from different angles.

First, from the side of physiology. This has given us the concept of *stimuli* and the scheme of the reflex arc, according to which a stimulus applied *from the outer world* to living tissue (nervous substance) is discharged by action *towards the outer world*. The action answers the purpose of withdrawing the substance affected from the operation of the stimulus, removing it out of range of the stimulus.

Now what is the relation between 'instinct' and 'stimulus'? There is nothing to prevent our including the concept of 'instinct' under that of 'stimulus' and saying that an instinct is a stimulus to the mind. But we are immediately set on our guard against treating instinct and mental stimulus as one and the same thing. Obviously, besides those of instinctual origin, there are other stimuli to the mind which behave far more like physiological stimuli. For example, a strong light striking upon the eye is not a stimulus of instinctual origin; it is one, however, when the mucous membrane of the œsophagus becomes parched or when a gnawing makes itself felt in the stomach.[1]

We have now obtained material necessary for discriminating between stimuli of instinctual origin and the other (physiological) stimuli which operate on our minds. First, a stimulus of instinctual origin does not arise in the outside world but from within the organism itself. For this reason it has a different mental effect and dif-

[1] Assuming, of course, that these internal processes constitute the organic basis of the needs described as thirst and hunger.

ferent actions are necessary in order to remove it. Further, all that is essential in an external stimulus is contained in the assumption that it acts as a single impact, so that it can be discharged by a single appropriate action—a typical instance being that of motor flight from the source of stimulation. Of course these impacts may be repeated and their force may be cumulative, but that makes no difference to our notion of the process and to the conditions necessary in order that the stimulus may be dispelled. An instinct, on the other hand, never acts as a momentary impact but always as a constant force. As it makes its attack not from without but from within the organism, it follows that no flight can avail against it. A better term for a stimulus of instinctual origin is a 'need'; that which does away with this need is 'satisfaction.' This can be attained only by a suitable (adequate) alteration of the inner source of stimulation.

Let us imagine ourselves in the position of an almost entirely helpless living organism, as yet unorientated in the world and with stimuli impinging on its nervous tissue. This organism will soon become capable of making a first discrimination and a first orientation. On the one hand, it will detect certain stimuli which can be avoided by an action of the muscles (flight)—these it ascribes to an outside world; on the other hand, it will also be aware of stimuli against which such action is of no avail and whose urgency is in no way diminished by it—these stimuli are the tokens of an inner world, the proof of instinctual needs. The apperceptive substance of the living organism will thus have found in the efficacy of its muscular activity a means for discriminating between 'outer' and 'inner.'

We thus find our first conception of the essential nature of an instinct by considering its main characteristics, its origin in sources of stimulation within the organism and its appearance as a constant force, and thence we deduce one of its further distinguishing features, namely, that no actions of flight avail against it. Now, in making these remarks, we cannot fail to be struck by a fact which compels us to a further admission. We do not merely accept as basal concepts certain conventions which we apply to the material we have acquired empirically, but we also make use of various complicated postulates to guide us in dealing with psychological phenomena. We have already cited the most important of these postulates; it remains for us expressly to lay stress upon it. It is of a biological nature, and makes use of the concept of 'purpose' (one might say, of adaptation of the means to the end) and runs as follows: the nervous system is an apparatus having the function of abolishing stimuli which reach it, or of reducing excitation to the lowest possible level: an apparatus which would even, if this were feasible, maintain itself in an altogether unstimulated condition. Let us for the present not take exception to the indefiniteness of this idea and let us grant that the task of the nervous system is—broadly speaking—*to master stimuli*. We see then how greatly the simple physiological reflex scheme is complicated by the introduction of instincts. External stimuli impose upon the organism the single task of withdrawing itself from their action: this is accomplished by muscular movements, one of which reaches the goal aimed at and, being the most appropriate to the end in view, is thenceforward transmitted as an hereditary disposition. Those instinctual stimuli which emanate from within the organism cannot be dealt with by this mechanism. Consequently, they make far higher demands upon the nervous system and compel it to complicated and interdependent activities, which effect such changes in the outer world as enable it to offer satisfaction to the internal source of stimulation; above all, instinctual stimuli oblige the nervous system to renounce its ideal intention of warding off stimuli, for they maintain an incessant and unavoidable afflux of stimulation. So we may probably conclude that instincts and not external stimuli are the true motive forces in the progress that has raised the nervous system, with all its incomparable efficiency, to its present high level of development. Of course there is nothing to prevent our assuming that the instincts themselves are, at least in part, the precipitates of different forms of external stimulation, which in the course of phylogenesis have effected modifications in the organism.

Then when we find further that the activity of even the most highly developed mental apparatus is subject to the pleasure-principle, *i.e.* is automatically regulated by feelings belonging to the pleasure-'pain' series, we can hardly reject the further postulate that these feelings reflect the manner in which the process of mastering stimuli takes place. This is certainly so in the sense that 'painful' feelings are connected with an increase and pleasurable feelings with a decrease in stimulation. Let us, however, be careful to preserve this assumption in its present highly indefinite form, until we succeed, if that is possible, in discovering what sort of relation exists between pleasure and 'pain,' on the one hand, and fluctuations in the quantities of stimuli affecting mental life, on the other. It is certain that many kinds of these relations are possible, some of them by no means simple.

If now we apply ourselves to considering mental life from a biological point of view, an 'instinct' appears to us as a borderland concept between the mental and the physical, being both the mental representative of the stimuli emanating from within the organism and penetrating to the mind, and at the same time a measure of the demand made upon the energy of the latter in consequence of its connection with the body.

We are now in a position to discuss certain terms used in reference to the concept of an instinct, for example, its impetus, its aim, its object and its source.

By the *impetus* of an instinct we understand its motor element, the amount of force or the measure of the demand upon energy which it represents. The characteristic of impulsion is common to all instincts, is in fact the very essence of them. Every instinct is a form of activity; if we speak loosely of passive instincts, we can only mean those whose aim is passive.

The *aim* of an instinct is in every instance satisfaction, which can only be obtained by abolishing the condition of stimulation in the source of the instinct. But although this remains invariably the final goal of every instinct, there may yet be different ways leading to the same goal, so that an instinct may be found to have various nearer or intermediate aims, capable of combination or interchange. Experience permits us also to speak of instincts which are *inhibited in respect of their aim*, in cases where a certain advance has been permitted in the direction of satisfaction and then an inhibition or deflection has occurred. We may suppose that even in such cases a partial satisfaction is achieved.

The *object* of an instinct is that in or through which it can achieve its aim. It is the most variable thing about an instinct and is not originally connected with it, but becomes attached to it only in consequence of being peculiarly fitted to provide satisfaction. The object is not necessarily an extraneous one: it may be part of the subject's own body. It may be changed any number of times in the course of the vicissitudes the instinct undergoes during life; a highly important part is played by this capacity for displacement in the instinct. It may happen that the same object may serve for the satisfaction of several instincts simultaneously, a phenomenon which Adler calls a 'confluence' of instincts. A particularly close attachment of the instinct to its object is distinguished by the term *fixation*: this frequently occurs in very early stages of the instinct's development and so puts an end to its mobility, through the vigorous resistance it sets up against detachment.

By the source of an instinct is meant that somatic process in an organ or part of the body from which there results a stimulus represented in mental life by an instinct. We do not know whether this process is regularly of a chemical nature or whether it may also correspond with the release of other, *e.g.* mechanical, forces. The study of the sources of instinct is outside the scope of psychology; although its source in the body is what gives the instinct its distinct and essential character, yet in mental life we know it merely by its aims. A more exact knowledge of the sources of instincts is not strictly necessary for purposes of psychological investigation; often the source may be with certainty inferred from the aims.

Are we to suppose that the different instincts which operate upon the mind but of which the origin is somatic are also distinguished by different qualities and act in the mental life in a manner qualitatively different? This supposition does not seem to be justified; we are much more likely to find the simpler assumption sufficient, namely, that the instincts are all qualitatively alike and owe the effect they produce only to the quantities of excitation accompanying them, or perhaps further to certain functions of this quantity. The difference in the mental effects produced by the different instincts may be traced to the difference in their sources. In any event, it is only in a later connection that we shall be able to make plain what the problem of the quality of instincts signifies.

Now what instincts and how many should be postulated? There is obviously a great opportunity here for arbitrary choice. No objection can be made to anyone's employing the concept of an instinct of play or of destruction, or that of a social instinct, when the subject demands it and the limitations of psychological analysis allow of it. Nevertheless, we should not neglect to ask whether such instinctual motives, which are in one direction so highly specialized, do not admit of further analysis in respect of their sources, so that only those primal instincts which are not to be resolved further could really lay claim to the name.

I have proposed that two groups of such primal instincts should be distinguished: the *self-preservative* or *ego*-instincts and the *sexual* instincts. But this proposition has not the weight of a necessary postulate, such as, for instance, our assumption about the biological 'purpose' in the mental apparatus (*v. supra*); it is merely an auxiliary construction, to be retained only so long as it proves useful, and it will make little difference to the results of our work of description and classification if we replace it by another. The occasion for it arose in the course of the evolution of psychoanalysis, which was first employed upon the psychoneuroses, actually upon the group designated transference neuroses (hysteria and obsessional neurosis); through them it became plain that at the root of all such affections there lies a conflict between the claims of sexuality and those of the ego. It is always possible that an exhaustive study of the other neurotic affections (especially of the narcissistic psychoneuroses, the schizophrenias) may oblige us to alter this formula and therewith to make a different classification of the primal instincts. But for the present we do not know what this new formula may be, nor have we met with any argument which seems likely to be prejudicial to the contrast between sexual and ego-instincts.

I am altogether doubtful whether work upon psychological material will afford any decisive indication for the distinction and classification of instincts. Rather it would seem necessary to apply to this material certain definite assumptions in order to work upon it, and we could wish that these assumptions might be taken from some other branch of knowledge and transferred to psychology. The contribution of biology on this point certainly does not run counter to the distinction between sexual and ego-instincts. Biology teaches that sexuality is not on a level with the other functions of the individual, for its 'purposes' go beyond the individual, their content being the production of new individuals and the preservation of the species. It shows, further, that the relation existing between the ego and sexuality may be conceived of in two ways, apparently equally well justified: in the one, the individual is regarded as of prime importance, sexuality as one of his activities and sexual satisfaction as one of his needs; while in the other the individual organism is looked upon as a transitory and perishable appendage to the quasi-immortal germ-plasm bequeathed to him by the race. The assumption that the sexual function differs from other bodily processes in virtue of special chemical processes is, I understand, also a postulate of the Ehrlich school of biological research.

Since a study of the instincts from the side of consciousness presents almost insuperable difficulties, psycho-analytic investigation of mental disturbances remains the principal source of our knowledge. The development of this line of investigation, however, has necessarily produced hitherto information of a more or less definite nature only in regard to the sexual instincts, for it is this group in particular which can be observed in isolation, as it were, in the psychoneuroses. With the extension of psycho-analysis to other neurotic affections we may be sure that we shall find a basis for our knowledge of the ego-instincts also, though it would be optimistic to expect equally favourable conditions for observation in this further field of research.

An attempt to formulate the general characteristics of the sexual instincts would run as follows: they are numerous, emanate from manifold organic sources, act in the first instance independently of one another and only at a late stage achieve a more or less complete synthesis. The aim which each strives to attain is 'organ-pleasure'; only when the synthesis is complete do they enter the service of the function of reproduction, becoming thereby generally recognizable as sexual instincts. At their first appearance they support themselves upon the instincts of self-preservation, from which they only gradually detach themselves; in their choice of object also they follow paths indicated by the ego-instincts. Some of them remain throughout life associated with these latter and furnish them with libidinal components, which with normal functioning easily escape notice and are clearly recognizable only when disease is present. They have this distinctive characteristic—that they have in a high degree the capacity to act vicariously for one another and that they can readily change their objects. In consequence of the last-mentioned properties they are capable of activities widely removed from their original modes of attaining their aims (sublimation).

2

The Hormic Psychology

WILLIAM McDOUGALL

Duke University

In the volume *Psychologies of 1925* I took the field as an exponent of *purposive psychology*. Anticipating a little the course of history, I shall here assume that the purposive nature of human action is no longer in dispute, and in this article shall endeavor to define and to justify that special form of purposive psychology which is now pretty widely known as *hormic psychology*. But first a few words in justification of this assumption.

Fifteen years ago American psychologists displayed almost without exception a complete blindness to the most peculiar, characteristic, and important feature of human and animal activity, namely, its goal-seeking. All bodily actions and all phases of experience were mechanical reactions to stimuli, and all learning was the modification of such reactions by the addition of one reaction to another according to the mechanical principles of association. The laws of learning were the laws of frequency, of recency, and of effect; and, though the law of effect as formulated by Thorndike may have suggested to some few minds that the mechanical principles involved were not so clear as might be wished, the laws of frequency and recency could give rise to no such misgivings. The law of effect, with its uncomfortable suggestion of an effect that somehow causes its cause, was pretty generally regarded as something to be got rid of by the substitution of some less ambiguous and more clearly mechanical formula.

Now, happily, all this is changed; the animal psy-

Reprinted from *Psychologies of 1930* edited by Carl Murchison, Clark University Press, 1930, with permission of the publishers.

chologists have begun to realize that any description of animal behavior which ignores its goal-seeking nature is futile, any "explanation" which leaves it out of account, factitious, and any experimentation which ignores motivation, grossly misleading; they are busy with the study of "drives," "sets," and "incentives." It is true that their recognition of goal-seeking is generally partial and grudging; they do not explicitly recognize that a "set" is a set toward an end, that a "drive" is an active striving toward a goal, that an "incentive" is something that provokes such active striving. The terms "striving" and "conation" are still foreign to their vocabularies.

Much the same state of affairs prevails in current American writings on human psychology. Its problems are no longer discussed, experiments are no longer made with total and bland disregard for the purposive nature of human activity. The terms "set," "drive," and "incentive," having been found indispensable in animal psychology, are allowed to appear in discussions of human problems, in spite of their anthropomorphic implications; "prepotent reflexes," "motives," "drives," "preponderant propensities," "impulses toward ends," "fundamental urges," and even "purposes" now figure in the text. In the final chapter on personality of a thoroughly mechanical text (1), in which the word "purpose" has been conspicuous by its absence, a rôle of first importance is assigned to "dominant purposes." Motivation, after being almost ignored, has become a problem of central interest. Yet, as was said above, we are in a transition period; and all this recognition of the purposive nature of human activity is partial and grudging. The author (Dr. H. A. Carr), who tells us on one page that "Man attempts to transform his environment to suit his own purposes," nowhere tells us what he means by the word "purposes" and is careful to tell us on a later page that "We must avoid the naïve assumption that the ulterior consequences of an act either motivate that act or serve as its objective." Almost without exception the authors who make any recognition of the goal-seeking or purposive nature of human and animal activities fall into one of the three following classes: (a) they imply that, if only we knew a little more about the nervous system, we should be able to explain such activities mechanically; or (b) they explicitly make this assertion; (c) more rarely, they proceed to attempt some such explanation.

Partial, half-hearted, reluctant as is still the recognition of purposive activity, it may, I think, fairly be said that only the crude behaviorists now ignore it completely; that, with that exception, American psychology has become purposive, in the sense that it no longer ignores or denies the goal-seeking nature of human and animal action, but accepts it as a problem to be faced.

It would, then, be otiose in this year of grace to defend or advocate purposive psychology in the vague sense of all psychology that recognizes purposiveness, takes account of foresight and of urges, impulses, cravings, desires, as motives of action.

My task is the more difficult one of justifying the far more radically purposive psychology denoted by the adjective "hormic," a psychology which claims to be autonomous; which refuses to be bound to and limited by the principles current in the physical sciences; which asserts that active striving towards a goal is a fundamental category of psychology, and is a process of a type that cannot be mechanistically explained or resolved into mechanistic sequences; which leaves it to the future development of the sciences to decide whether the physical sciences shall continue to be mechanistic or shall find it necessary to adopt hormic interpretations of physical events, and whether we are to have ultimately one science of nature, or two, the mechanistic and the teleological. For hormic psychology is not afraid to use teleological description and explanation. Rather, it insists that those of our activities which we can at all adequately describe are unmistakably and undeniably teleological, are activities which we undertake in the pursuit of some goal, for the sake of some result which we foresee and desire to achieve. And it holds that such activities are the true type of all mental activities and of all truly vital activities, and that, when we seek to interpret more obscure instances of human activity and when we observe on the part of animals actions that clearly are goal-seeking, we are well justified in regarding them as of the same order as our own explicitly teleological or purposive actions.

While the academic psychologies of the recent past have sought to explain the higher types of activity from below upward, taking simple physical and chemical events as their starting-point, hormic psychology begins by accepting the higher activities, those which are clearly and explicitly purposive and into the nature of which we have the most insight, and seeks to extend such insight downwards to the simpler but more obscure types of action.

TELEOLOGY, INTRINSIC AND EXTRINSIC

I introduce the term 'teleological' early in the exposition because I do not wish to seem to smuggle it in at a later stage after betraying the innocent reader into acceptance of a position which commits him unwittingly to teleology. Modern science has shown an aversion to all teleology; one might almost say that it has a 'complex' on that subject. The origin and development of this unreasoning and unreasonable aversion is intelligible enough. It developed in the course of the conflict of science with religion. The favorite explanation of all obscure natural processes offered by the theologians was that they expressed and were governed by the purpose of the Creator, who had designed and constructed the various objects of the natural world in order that, as parts of one grand system, they might exhibit and fulfil His purposes. Whether the theologians conceived natural objects as having been once and for all designed and created in such a way that natural events would run their courses, fulfilling God's purpose without further intervention on His part, or believed that the finger of God still actively directs the course of natural events, these teleological explanations were, in either case, utterly repugnant to the spirit of modern science; for science had found it possible to explain many events as the effects of natural causes, and it had become the accepted program of science to extend such explanations as widely as possible.

It has become usual to speak of the explanations offered by science as naturalistic, and to oppose them to the supernatural explanations of the theologians.

Now, to explain an event is to assign the causes of it, the play of antecedent events of which the event in question is the consequence. Early scientists inclined to interpret many events after the model of our own experience of causation. We foresee a particular event as a possibility; we desire to see this possibility realized; we take action in accordance with our desire, and we seem to guide the course of events in such a way that the foreseen and desired event results. To explain an event as caused in this way was to invoke teleological causation, not the extrinsic supernatural teleology of the theologians, but a natural teleological causation, a causal activity thoroughly familiar to each man through his own repeated experiences of successful action for the attainment of desired goals. Primitive man applied explanation of this type to many natural events, regarding anthropomorphically many natural objects which modern science has taught us to regard as utterly devoid of any such affinity with ourselves. The early students of physical nature did not entirely discard explanations of this type. They regarded natural events more analytically than primitive men had done; but they still inclined to regard the elements into which they analyzed the given natural objects as acting teleologically, as moved by desire, and as striving to achieve the effects they naturally desired. The Newtonian mechanics put an end to explanation of this type in the physical sciences. For it appeared that very many physical events, more especially various astronomical events, could be adequately explained in terms of mass, motion, momentum, attraction, and repulsion, all exactly measurable; and many such events became strictly predictable from such principles of causation. From such causal explanations all reference to foresight of something, to desire for something, to striving for that something, in fact all reference to the future course of events, was wholly excluded. The explanation of any event was given in terms only of other events antecedent to it; all reference to possible or probable consequences proved to be unnecessary; explanation was purged of all taint of teleology. Explanation of this type was so successful in the physical sciences that, although the hope of strictly mechanical explanation of all events of the

inanimate world is now seen
ateleological explanation has
type and model to which natu
conform. Such ateleological exp.
by mechanistic explanation in ur
mechanistic or ateleological explana.
dubbed naturalistic and were accepted in ...... of
supernatural teleological explanations of theology. So
far all was well; the procedure was entirely justified. But
at this point an unfortunate confusion of thought became very general. The confusion consisted in falling
victim to the compelling force of words and in regarding
as supernatural, not only the external teleological causation of the theologians, but also the internal teleological
causation or causal activity of men.

This, I say, was an unfortunate and unwarranted confusion; and it still pervades the thinking of most men of
science when they approach the problems of psychology
and biology. Any proposal to take seriously the teleological causation which seems to be revealed in human
activities, to regard such causation as real and effective,
they repudiate as trafficking in supernatural causes; for,
in learning to repudiate the external supernatural teleology of theology, they have come to regard as also
supernatural the internal teleological causation of the
human organism. Yet there is no good ground for so regarding it. To desire, to strive, and to attain our goal is
as natural as falling off a log, and with such teleological
causation we are entirely familiar; we have more intimate
understanding of it than of mechanistic causation.

During the nineteenth century, under the prevalence
of the faith that strictly mechanical or Newtonian causation was adequate to the explanation of all events of the
inanimate world, it was natural enough to regard such
causation as the one and only type of naturalistic causation, and, therefore, to class intrinsic teleological causation with the extrinsic teleological causation of the

[1] As I have shown in my *Modern Materialism and Emergent
Evolution* (21), there is no other way of defining the meaning
of the word "mechanistic," no other way than this negative
way which defines it by excluding all trace of teleology, all
reference to the future; mechanistic means ateleological.

as supernatural. But now, when it has be-
that that faith or hope was illusory and that
ve no insight into the nature of mechanistic causa-
on, this ground for repudiating internal teleological
causation has been taken away—and none remains.

It is probable that the remaining prejudice against it is
more than a hang-over from the days of belief in strictly
mechanical or Newtonian causation. To accept the teleological causation of human agents is to believe in the
causal efficacy of psychical events; and it seems to be
widely felt that to do this is necessarily to commit one's
self to psychophysical dualism or animism, and thus to
offend against the common preference for a monistic
world-view and against the theory of continuity of evolution of the organic from the inorganic. But this is an
error which a little clear thinking should quickly dispel.
Two monistic theories, both implying continuity of
evolution, are now enjoying considerable vogue among
both philosophers and men of science, namely, psychic
monism and the emergent theory.

Psychic monism, as expounded by Paulsen, Morton
Prince, C. A. Strong, Durant Drake, and L. T. Troland,
has no ground for doubting the causal efficacy of psychic
events; for its teaching is that all events are psychic.
Morton Prince, with his ever youthful mind, saw this
clearly enough and hence did not hesitate to figure as an
exponent of purposive psychology in the volume *Psychologies of 1925* (27). Dr. Troland, curiously enough,
seems to cast aside in the most gratuitous fashion the
opportunity afforded by his espousal of psychic monism
to lift psychology above the sterile plane of mechanistic
explanation.

The emergent theory[2] is equally compatible with, and
in fact asserts, the causal efficacy of psychic events and
the continuity of organic with inorganic evolution; and
it is a monistic theory. Hence it fulfils all the requirements of the psychologist who cannot blind himself to

[2] Cf. Lloyd Morgan's two volumes of Gifford Lectures,
Emergent Evolution (24) and *Life, Mind and Spirit* (25),
also my *Modern Materialism and Emergent Evolution* (21)
for exposition of the emergent theory.

the reality of goal-seeking behavior and purposive activity, and yet holds fast to monism and continuity of evolution. And it is a theory now in excellent standing, sponsored by such outstanding thinkers as S. Alexander, L. T. Hobhouse, Lloyd Morgan, H. S. Jennings, R. B. Perry, W. M. Wheeler.

With these alternatives open to the choice of the psychologist, he has no valid ground for denying the causal efficacy of psychic activity in the natural world, no ground for continuing to regard internal teleological causation as supernatural, and therefore no ground for blinding himself to the purposive nature of human activity. One suspects that the prevalent reluctance to recognize fully and freely the purposive nature of human activity and the goal-seeking nature of animal activities is mainly due to the fact that most of us were brought up to believe in epiphenomenalism of psychophysical parallelism, those equally illogical, profoundly unsatisfactory, and now discredited makeshifts of a generation dominated by mechanical materialism and imbued with an ill-founded prejudice in favor of regarding all causation as mechanistic. Or perhaps the common case is simpler: throughout a considerable period the physical sciences have worked very successfully in terms of purely mechanistic or ateleological causation; therefore psychology and all the biological sciences must do likewise. To this contention the answer is obvious: this policy is running psychology and biology in general into a blind alley. Weismannism, the only purely mechanistic theory of biological evolution, has broken down; and vague theories of creative evolution or othogenesis are the order of the day. There is renewed interest in the possibility of Lamarckian transmission. Physiologists are breaking away from the mechanistic tradition. Dr. K. S. Lashley, in his presidential address to the American Psychological Association, speaking in the light of his own very extensive researches, has thrown all the prevailing views on cerebral action back into the melting-pot without offering a substitute. Three at least of the leaders of biology in America, Lillie, Herrick, and Jennings, are calling aloud for recognition of the causal efficacy in nature of psychical activities.[3] In Great Britain, Drs. J. S. Haldane and E. S. Russell are building up the psychobiological school, which utterly denies the adequacy of mechanistic principles of explanation in biology. (The former bluntly denounces as "claptrap" the claim, so often repeated "parrot-like," that physiology is revealing the mechanism of life.) The German thinkers interested in the various human sciences, impatient of the failure of the "strictly scientific" psychology taught in the universities to furnish any psychological basis for those sciences, are turning away to construct a psychology of the kind they need, a *geisteswissenschaftliche Psychologie*, which frankly throws aside the mechanistic principles and recognizes the teleological nature of human activity. The Gestalt school of psychology protests against mechanistic interpretations.

Clearly the dominance of biology by the mechanistic ideal of the physical sciences is passing; while physical science itself is giving up strict determinism and exact

[3] Dr. R. S. Lillie (11) writes: "What we agree to call the spiritual appears at times to act directly as a transformer of the physical, as in artistic or other creation. Such experiences cannot be accounted for on physical grounds, for one reason because it is in the very nature of physical abstraction to rule out as irrelevant all factors of a volitional or other 'psychic' kind. To trace the course of the physiological processes accompanying an act of intellectual creation would undoubtedly give us curious information, of a kind, but would throw little if any light on the essential nature of the reality underlying."

Dr. C. J. Herrick (5) writes: "No abyss of ignorance of what consciousness really is, no futilities of introspective analysis, no dialectic, destroy the simple datum that I have conscious experience and that this experience is a controlling factor in my behavior. . . . The prevision of possible future consequences of action is a real causative factor in determining which course of action will actually be chosen." Cf. also (6).

H. S. Jennings is no less emphatic. He writes (9) of "that monstrous absurdity that has so long been a reproach to biological science; the doctrine that ideas, ideals, purposes have no effect on behavior. The mental determines what happens as does any other determiner. . . . The desires and aspirations of humanity are determiners in the operation of the universe on the same footing with physical determiners."

predictability. Where, then, is to be found any justification for the old-fashioned prejudice against psychical
causation, which, if admitted at all, can be only teleological causation? Why should not we psychologists,
whose business is with the psychical, boldly claim that
here is the indeterminate and creative element in nature,
rather than leave it to physicists and physiologists to
show the way and force us to recognize the fact? To
admit the efficacy of psychical activity in nature is not,
as so many seem to imagine, to deny causation.[4] Science

[4] E.g., Professor R. S. Woodworth (33) writes: "Some authors, as especially McDougall, appear to teach that any thor-
ough-going causal interpretation of human behavior and experience implies shutting one's eyes to the facts of purpose and
striving. There is certainly some confusion here. There can be
no contradiction between the purposiveness of a sequence of
action and its being a causal sequence. A purpose is certainly
a cause: if it had no effect, it would be without significance."
There is confusion here; but I suggest it is Woodworth's thinking, rather than mine, that is confused. Both in this essay and
in his Psychology (34), Woodworth professes to give full recognition to "purpose" and even says, as in the passage cited,
that a purpose is a cause. To me it seems very misleading to
speak either of "a purpose" or of "a cause." And the sentence,
"a purpose is a cause," is ambiguous and confused; it leaves the
reader in doubt of the author's meaning. We go in search of
passages which will tell what the author means by "a purpose."
We find in the same essay that "Your purpose would be futile
if it had no effects, it would be incredible if it had no causes.
It is a link in a causal chain, but it is as fine a purpose for all
that." Now, in the same essay, Woodworth characteristically
refuses to face the question of what he calls "the philosophy
of purpose and striving and their place in the world-process as
a whole," as also the question of the validity of the mechanistic
conception of life. He will not commit himself for or against
the mechanistic conception. He seeks to give the impression
that his psychology takes full account of the purposive striving
of men and animals. He would like to run with the hare and
hunt with the hounds; he desires both to eat his cake and to
have it. He is too clear-sighted to ignore the facts of goal-
seeking; but his thinking is too timid to allow him to see and
to say that here is a parting of the ways, a crucial question to
which one of two answers is right and the other wrong, the
question, namely—Is human mental activity mechanistic or is
it teleological? However these two terms be defined (and as I

must hold fast to causation, if not to strict determination. Psychical events, though teleological, have their conditions and their causal antecedents; but in them the foreseeing activity is a real factor which makes, not the fu-

---

have said, the only satisfactory way of defining "mechanistic process" is the negative one of defining it as the ateleological), they are by common consent mutually exclusive: if a process is mechanistic, it is not teleological; and if it is teleological, it is not mechanistic. But in spite of Woodworth's careful noncommittal ambiguity, and in spite of his air of giving full recognition to the causal efficacy of purposive striving, it seems that he remains mechanistic; that he means by cause and causation always and only the mechanistic type, and means to repudiate all teleological causation. This comes to light in one passage: he writes of a "need" as "the controlling factor in the activity"; and immediately adds: "Whether the concept of 'need' is a useful dynamic concept is perhaps open to doubt; it smacks considerably of the sort of teleology that we do well to leave aside." Even here he suggests vaguely that there is teleology of some sort that he would not leave aside; but that is merely one more expression of his inveterate tendency to sit on the fence. When we discover finally his definition of "a purpose," it confirms our suspicion that, in spite of all his well-sounding camouflage, Woodworth is on the side of the mechanists: "Conscious purpose is an adjustment still in the making or just being tuned up, and specially an adjustment that is broad and still precise. . . . Purpose is the activity itself, initiated but not completed. It is an activity in progress." Again: "A purpose is a set for a certain activity with foresight of the result of that activity." But does the foresight play any part, or is it merely an accompaniment? Woodworth refuses to commit himself. "How can a conscious purpose have any effect on the brain and muscles anyway? Thus one of the old puzzles of philosophy is injected into our peaceful psychological study, muddling our heads and threatening to wreck our intellectual honesty. We cannot deal with this metaphysical question here" (34). Woodworth would like to explain human action teleologically; but he sees that to do so would be to admit the causal efficacy of psychical activity, and, as he cannot bring himself to take that step, his intellectual "honesty" compels him to put the responsibility on the metaphysicians until such time as the push from his scientific colleagues of the other sciences shall leave him and his fellow-psychologists no option in the matter.

ture event foreseen, but the foreseeing of it as possible
and as desirable or repugnant a cooperating factor in the
total configuration of the present moment. To put it in
other words, valuation is a psychical function which is
rooted in the past history of the individual and of the
race; and it is an activity that makes a difference; applied
to the foreseen possibility, it inclines our activity this way
or that, to seek or accept, avoid or reject.

Surely, a future age, looking back upon the vagaries of
our own, will record with astonishment the fact that in
this early stage of the development of the biological
sciences, men of science, while perceiving clearly that
the power of foreseeing, of anticipating the future course
of events, has developed steadily in the race until in man
it has become his most striking characteristic, yet persistently deny that this wonderful capacity is of any service in our struggle for existence.[5]

[5] Many eminent physicians have insisted on the control and
direction of energy transformations by human agency as something that will not fit with the physicists' scheme of things.
Why, then, should psychologists fear to follow them? I cite
a very recent instance. Commenting on Eddington's discussion
of the law of entropy as universally valid in the physical realm,
Sir O. Lodge (12) writes: "This has long been known, but
Eddington illustrates it very luminously by what he calls the
operation of 'shuffling.' Given an orderly pack of cards, it may
be hopelessly disorganized by shuffling, and no amount of
shuffling will bring it back into order. [It is pointless to say, as
does a recent reviewer of Eddington's book, that, if you continue to shuffle for an infinite time, the order will be restored;
for the order may be restored by human activity many times in
a brief period.] Many of the processes in nature thus result in
greater disorganization; and, according to Eddington, the ir-
reversible disorganization measures the entropy. Entropy is
disorganization. It is easy to break an orderly arrangement
down, but not so easy to build it up. Yet it can be built up.
Not by random and unintelligent processes truly: a mob of
monkeys playing on a million typewriters will not compose a
volume of poems. The only way to restore order is to apply
the activity of mind. . . . Shuffling, as Eddington luminously
says, is 'an absent-minded operation.' . . . Mind is essential
to organization, and organization or reorganization is a *natural
result of mental activity consciously directed to a present end.*"

TWO FORMS OF TELEOLOGICAL OR PURPOSIVE
PSYCHOLOGY, THE HEDONISTIC AND THE HORMIC

The psychologist who can summon enough courage to
follow the lead of physicists and biologists and to accept
the causal efficacy of psychical activity, of foresight and
desire, is confronted with a choice between two theories
of the ground of all desire, of all striving or conation,
the hedonistic and the hormic.

Psychological hedonism enjoyed a great vogue in the
nineteenth century and is not yet dead; for it embodies
some truth. Not every theory of action that assigns a rôle
to pleasure and pain is teleological. Two prominent
American psychologists, Drs. E. L. Thorndike and L. T.
Troland, have elaborated a theory which remains strictly
mechanistic, though it assigns a rôle to pleasure and pain.
In this theory, pleasure accompanying any form of activity "stamps in" that activity, affects the brain structures in such a way that similar activity is the more likely
to recur under similar conditions; and pain has the opposite effect. It is clear that there is nothing teleological
in this form of hedonic theory; it is a hedonism of the
past. It is a striking evidence of the strength of the
prejudice against teleological causation, that Dr. Troland,
who believes that all things and events are in reality psychical, should thus choose to eleborate his psychical theory in terms of purely mechanistic causation.[6]

[6] Cf. (31). Dr. C. J. Herrick (7) follows the same strange
procedure. He stoutly asserts the causal efficacy of psychical
events, especially of ideals, but just as decidedly proclaims the
all-sufficiency of mechanistic principles in biology and psychology. Like Woodworth (cf. footnote 4), he seems to believe
that to admit the teleological causation involved in the working
of an ideal would be to give up causation. His unexamined
postulate is that the natural is the mechanistic, and any non-
mechanistic or teleological causation is *ipso facto* non-natural
or supernatural. He accepts emergent evolution and asserts that
the human brain is a creative agent; yet asserts also that it
works purely mechanistically. He does not see that these two
assertions are in flat contradiction, that a strictly mechanistic
event cannot be creative of novelties; that to assert it to be so
is to make a self-contradictory statement, since "mechanistic"
excludes "creation of novelty" in its definition.

A second form of hedonism ma͟
of the present." It asserts that all ac
as prompted by the pleasure or the ͟
of experience. Its position in relation
teleology is ambiguous. It can be hel͟
mechanistic form: the feeling accom͟
process is a factor of causal efficacy in the ͟ ͟ura-
tion, one that prolongs and modifies the ͟ ͟ process.
It can be stated in a teleological form: the pleasure of the
moment prompts efforts to prolong the pleasurable activity and secure more pleasure; the pain of the present
moment prompts an effort to get rid of the pain and
secure ease. In this second form the rôle assigned to foresight renders the formulation teleological.

This second variety of hedonism embodies truth. But
it is false if put forward as a general theory of all action.
We do seek to prolong pleasant activities and to get rid
of pain. But it is not true that all, or indeed any large
proportion, of our activities can be explained in this way.
Our seeking of a goal, our pursuit of an end, is an activity that commonly incurs pleasure or pain; but these
are incidental consequences. Our striving after food, or a
mate, or power, knowledge, revenge, or relief of others'
suffering is commonly but little influenced by the hedonic
effects incident to our striving. The conation is prior to,
and not dependent upon, its hedonic accompaniments,
though these may and do modify its course.

The traditional psychological hedonism is thoroughly
teleological. It asserts that all human action is performed
for the sake of attaining a foreseen pleasure or of avoiding foreseen pain. It is, however, inacceptable, and for
two reasons chiefly. First, it is in gross contradiction with
clear instances of human action initiated and sustained,
not only without anticipation of resulting pleasure or of
resulting avoidance of pain, but with clear anticipation of
a resulting excess of pain. Secondly, it cannot be applied
to the interpretation of animal action (unless, possibly, to
some actions of the highest animals); and thus would
make between human and animal action a radical difference of principle, inconsistent with the well-founded

of continuity of human with animal evolution.[7] The hopeless inadequacy of psychological hedonism appears very clearly when it is attempted to apply it to the explanation of our valuations. J. S. Mill attempted to extricate the doctrine from its predicament in face of the problem of values by recognizing lower and higher pleasures; but it is generally conceded that in so doing he saved his moral theory at the cost of making an indefensible psychological distinction.

It should be sufficient answer to point to that sphere of human experience which the hedonists most commonly adduce in illustration of their theory, namely, the sexual. When we reflect on the profound influence of the sex urge in human life, its vast range, its immeasurable strength that so often drives men to the most reckless adventures and the most tragic disasters or sustains them through immense and prolonged labors, its frenzies of passionate desire, its lofty exaltations and its deep depressions, we must surely conclude that he who would see the ground of all these phenemona in the pleasurable tone of certain cutaneous sensations must lack all personal experience of any but the most trivial manifestations of sex.

THE HORMIC THEORY OF ACTION

We are thus driven to the hormic theory as the only alternative teleological theory of action. The essence of it may be stated very simply. To the question—Why does a certain animal or man seek this or that goal?—it replies: Because it is his nature to do so. This answer, simple as it may seem, has deep significance.

[7] The fallacy that hedonism can explain both human and animal actions involves, I suggest, a confusion of teleological hedonism, the theory that we act for the sake of attaining pleasure or of avoiding pain, with mechanistic hedonism, the theory that pleasures and pains leave after-effects which play their parts in the determination of subsequent actions, and with hedonism-of-the-present, the theory that pleasure sustains present action and pain checks or turns it aside. The first is used to explain human action; the second or third, or both, to explain animal action.

Observation of animals of any one species shows that all members of the species seek and strive toward a limited number of goals of certain types, certain kinds of food and of shelter, their mates, the company of their fellows, certain geographical areas at certain seasons, escape to cover in presence of certain definable circumstances, dominance over their fellows, the welfare of their young, and so on. For any one species the kinds of goals sought are characteristic and specific; and all members of the species seek these goals independently of example and of prior experience of attainment of them, though the course of action pursued in the course of striving towards the goal may vary much and may be profoundly modified by experience. We are justified, then, in inferring that each member of the species inherits the tendencies of the species to seek goals of these several types.

Man also is a member of an animal species. And this species also has its natural goals, or its inborn tendencies to seek goals of certain types. This fact is not only indicated very clearly by any comparison of human with animal behavior, but it is so obvious a fact that no psychologist of the least intelligence fails to recognize it, however inadequately, not even if he obstinately reduces their number to a minimum of three and dubs them the "prepotent reflexes" of sex, fear, and rage. Others write of "primary desires," or of "dominant urges," or of "unconditioned reflexes," or of appetites, or of cravings, or of congenital drives, or of motor sets, or of inherited tendencies or propensities; lastly, some, bolder than the rest, write of "so-called instincts." For instincts are out of fashion just now with American psychologists; and to write of instincts without some such qualification as "so-called" betrays a reckless indifference to fashion amounting almost to indecency. Yet the word "instinct" is too good to be lost to our science. Better than any other word it points to the facts and the problems with which I am here concerned.

The hormic psychology imperatively requires recognition not only of instinctive action but of instincts. Primarily and traditionally the words "instinct" and "instinctive" point to those types of animal action which are complex activities of the whole organism; which lead the creature to the attainment of one or other of the goals natural to the species; which are in their general nature manifested by all members of the species under appropriate circumstances; which exhibit nice adaptation to circumstances; and which, though often suggesting intelligent appreciation of the end to be gained and the means to be adopted, yet owe little or nothing to the individual's prior experience.[8]

[8] Two very different prejudices have cooperated to give currency in recent psychology to a very perverted and misleading view of instinctive action. On the one hand are those observers of animal life (of whom Fabre and Wasmann are the most distinguished) whose religious philosophy forbids them to admit the essential and close similarities between human and animal actions. Thus prejudiced, they select and emphasize all their observations and reports of animal, and especially of insect, behavior the stereotyped unvarying instances, those which seem to imply lack of all individual adaptation to unusual situations. Thus they emphasize the quasi-mechanical character of instinctive behavior.

On the other hand, the mechanists, moved by the desire to find instinctive actions mechanically explicable, also select and emphasize these same instances and aspects, neglecting to notice the very numerous and striking evidences of adaptability of instinctive action in ways that can only be called intelligent. Thus both parties are led into regarding instinctive behavior as always a train of action precisely predetermined in the innate constitution of the animal. And this view, of course, readily lends itself to interpretation of all instinctive action as the mechanistic play of chains of reflexes, the touching-off by stimuli of so-called "action-patterns" congenitally formed in the nervous system.

Yet any impartial review of instinctive behavior [an excellent example is Major R. W. G. Hingston's recent book (8)] shows clearly the falsity of this view, shows beyond dispute that instinctive action (even among the insects) does not consist in any rigidly prescribed sequence of movements, and that any particular type of instinctive behavior cannot be characterized by the particular movements and sequences of movements but only by the type of goal towards which the action is directed. Any such review reveals clearly two much neglected facts: (1) that very different instincts of the one animal may express themselves in very similar trains of movement; (2) that one instinct may express itself in a great variety of movements. A dog racing along with utmost concentration of energy in the

The words as thus traditionally used point to a problem. The word "instinctive" describes actions of this type. The word "instinct" implies that unknown something which expresses itself in the train of instinctive action directed towards a particular natural goal. What is the nature of that x to which the word "instinct" points? The problem has provoked much speculation all down the ages; the answers ranging from 'the finger of God' to 'a rigid bit of reflex nervous mechanism.'

It is characteristic of the hormic theory that it does not presume to give a final and complete answer to this question in terms of entities of types of events that enjoy well-established scientific status.

Hormic activity is an energy manifestation; but the hormic theory does not presume to say just what form or forms of energy or transformations of energy are involved. It seems to involve liberation of energy potential or latent in chemical form in the tissues; and hormic theory welcomes any information about such transformations that physiological chemistry can furnish. But it refuses to go beyond the facts and to be bound by current hypotheses of physical science; and it refuses to be

---

effort of speedy locomotion may be pursuing his prey; he may be fleeing from a larger pursuing dog or leopard; or he may be rushing to join a concourse of dogs. On the other hand, in either fighting or pursuing and seizing his prey, he may bring into play a very large proportion of his total capacities for coordinated movement, his native motor mechanisms; and many of the motor mechanisms which he brings into play are identical in the two cases. Or consider the male pigeon in the two very different instinctive activities of fighting and courting; the forms of bodily activity he displays are in many respects so similar that an inexperienced observer may be unable to infer which instinct is at work in him. In both, all the motor mechanisms of locomotion and of self-display, of flying, strutting, walking, running, and vocalization, are in turn brought into action; few, if any, of the many motor manifestations are peculiar to the expression of either instinct. These facts are very difficult to interpret in terms of neurology; but that difficulty does not justify us in denying or ignoring them. The tendency to deny or ignore the many facts of behavior that present this difficulty has long been dominant in American psychology and is a bar to progress of the first magnitude.

blinded to the essential facts. And the most essential facts are (a) that the energy manifestation is guided into channels such that the organism approaches its goal; (b) that this guidance is effected through a cognitive activity, an awareness, however vague, of the present situation and of the goal; (c) that the activity, once initiated and set on its path through cognitive activity, tends to continue until the goal is attained; (d) that, when the goal is attained, the activity terminates; (e) that progress towards and attainment of the goal are pleasurable experiences, and thwarting and failure are painful or disagreeable experiences.

These statements imply that hormic activity is essentially mental activity, involving always cognition or awareness, striving initiated and governed by such cognition, and accruing satisfaction or dissatisfaction. The theory holds that these are three fundamental aspects of all hormic activity, distinguishable by abstraction, but not separable or capable of occurring in nature as separate events. Thus it necessarily holds that hormic activity can be exhibited only by organisms or natural entities that have a certain complexity of organization, such entities as have been traditionally called monads. And it inclines to the view that the simplest form under which such monads appear to us as sensible phenomena is that of the single living cell. The theory does not seek to explain the genesis of such complex organizations by the coming together of simpler entities. It inclines to regard any attempt at such a genetic account (such, for example, as has been attempted by various exponents of emergent evolution) as inevitably fruitless: for it regards with extreme scepticism the common assumption that every thing and event can in principle be analyzed into some complex of ultimately simple things and events; and it is especially sceptical of the emergentists' assumption that a conjunction of purely mechanistic events can result in the emergence of teleological events.[9]

The theory is ready to welcome and accept any evidence which physical science can furnish of hormic

[9] Cf. my *Modern Materialism and Emergent Evolution* (21).

activity, however lowly, in the inorganic sphere, and is ready to use such evidence to build a bridge between the organic and the inorganic realms; but it is content to await the verdict of the physicists, confident that its own facts and formulations will stand fast whether that verdict prove to be positive or negative. In short, the hormic theory holds that where there is life there is mind; and that, if there has been continuity of evolution of the organic from the inorganic, there must have been something of mind, some trace of mental nature and activity in the inorganic from which such emergence took place.

THE ADEQUACY OF THE HORMIC THEORY

The question arises: Is the hormic theory as here stated adequate to the interpretation of all forms of animal and human activity? And the question takes two forms: First, can the hormic theory be carried over from psychology into physiology? Can it be profitably applied to the interpretation of the activities of the several organs and tissues? This is a very deep question which only the future course of science can answer. But we notice that biologists are becoming increasingly conscious of the inadequacy of mechanistic principles to their problems, especially the problems of evolution, of heredity, of self-regulation, of the maintenance of organic equilibrium, of the restitution of forms and functions after disturbance of the normal state of affairs in the organism, and are seeing that, as Dr. E. S. Russell (29) emphatically insists, "the essential difference between the inorganic unit and the living individual is that the activities of all living things tend toward some end and are not easily diverted from achieving this end . . . all goes on in the organic world as if living beings strove actively towards an end . . . what differentiates a living thing from all inorganic objects or units is this persistence of striving, this effort towards the expression of deep-lying distinctive tendencies." We therefore are all well disposed to agree with this physiologist when he writes: "We must interpret all organic activities as in some sense the actions of a psychophysical individual." [10] That is to say, we may reasonably hope that it may become increasingly possible to extend the hormic principle to the elucidation of fundamental problems of physiology and of general biology.

Secondly, are the inborn impulses (*die Triebe*) the only sources of motive power? For this is the thesis of the hormic theory in the pure form as propounded in my *Social Psychology* in 1908 (13). Let me cite a restatement of it by Professor James Drever of Edinburgh (2). "The basis of the developed mind and character of man must be sought in the original and inborn tendencies of his nature. From these all development and education must start, and with these all human control, for the purposes of education and development, as for the purposes of social and community life, must operate. These are more or less truisms, but they are truisms which have been ignored in much of the educational practice of the past, and in many of the best intentioned efforts at social reorganization and reform. The original human nature, with which the psychologist is concerned, consists, first of

---

[10] Dr. J. S. Haldane (3), distinguished as one of the most exact of experimental physiologists, referring to the notion that life and mind may have emerged from a lifeless and mindless, strictly mechanistic realm, writes: "I must frankly confess that to me it seems that such ideas are not clearly thought out. In fact they convey to me no meaning whatever. It is very different, however, if we conclude that in spite of superficial appearances something of conscious behavior must in reality be present behind what appears to us as the mere blind organic behavior of lower organisms or plants," to which he adds, though on very different grounds—behind also "what appears to be the mere mechanical behaviour of the inorganic world." In the same volume he rightly insists: "The knowledge represented in the psychological or humanistic group of sciences is not only differentiated clearly from other kinds of scientific knowledge, but is the most fundamental variety of scientific knowledge." He adds: "I am thoroughly convinced of the limitations attached to physiological interpretation of human behaviour. At present there is what seems to me an exaggerated idea among the general public, not of the importance of psychological knowledge, for its importance can hardly be overestimated, but of the importance of mere physiological or even physical treatment of human behaviour."

all, of capacities, such as the capacity to have sensations, to perceive, to reason, to learn, and the like, and, secondly, of conscious impulses, the driving forces to those activities without which the capacities would be meaningless." And "though control of primitive impulses becomes more and more complex, it is always a control by that which draws its controlling force, ultimately and fundamentally, from primitive impulses, never a control *ab extra*." Yet again: "Educationally the most important fact to keep in mind with regard to these specific 'emotional' tendencies is that in them we have . . . the original, and ultimately the sole important, motive forces determining an individual's behavior, the sole original determinants of the ends he will seek to attain, as of the interests which crave satisfaction."

If my knowledge of contemporary thought is not gravely at fault, four and only four attempts to supplement the pure hormic theory as here concisely stated call for consideration.

First, we have to consider a view maintained by Professor Drever himself, inconsistently as it seems to me, with his statements cited in the foregoing paragraphs. He writes in the same treatise: "It must be granted that, in the human being, in addition to the instinctive springs of action, or motive forces which determine behavior prior to individual experience, pleasure and pain are also motive forces depending upon individual experience" (2, p. 149). To admit this is to combine hedonism with hormism; and in such combination Dr. Drever does not stand alone; he is in the good company of Professor S. Freud and all his many disciples.

I take Dr. Drever's statement to mean that man learns to anticipate pain or pleasure from this or that form of activity and in consequence to turn away from the former and to choose the latter. Now, in so far as we have in view the modes of activity adopted or followed as means to our goals, this is certainly true doctrine. Past experiences of pain and pleasure attending our activities are remembered; they determine our anticipations of pain and pleasure; and we choose our forms of activity, our lines of approach to our goals, in accordance with such anticipations. But more than this is implied in the statement that "pleasure and pain are also motive forces," as also in Freud's "pleasure principle." It is implied that desire of pleasure and the aversion from pain are motive forces which impel us to goals independently of the hormic impulses. It is a mixed theory of action, which supplements the hormic theory with a measure of hedonism. Is this true? Does the hormic theory require this admixture? The answer seems clear in the case of pain. The anticipation of pain from a certain course of action can only deter from that line of activity; it turns us not from the goal of that activity, but only from the form of activity previously followed in pursuit of that goal; and, if we can find no other line of activity that promises attainment, we may in the end cease to strive toward that goal; but the anticipation of the pain is not in itself a motive to action. Pain in the proper sense is always the accompaniment or consequence of thwarting of desire, of failure of impulse or effort; and, if we desire nothing, if we strive after no goals, we shall suffer no pains. This is the great truth underlying the Buddhist philosophy of renunciation.

There is one seeming exception that arises from the ambiguity of language; the word "pain" is applied not only to feeling that results from thrwarting and failure but also to a specific quality or qualities of sensation. And we are accustomed to regard "pain-sensation" as a spur to action, and also the aversion from anticipated "pain-sensation" as a motive to activity the goal of which is the avoidance of such "pain." Here is a grand source of confusion; which, however, is cleared away forthwith when we recognize the fact that pain-sensation from any part of the body is a specific excitant of fear, and fear is or involves a powerful hormic impulse.

It is notorious that threats of physical punishment, if they are to spur the unwilling child or man to activity, must be pushed to the point of exciting fear in him; short of that they are of no avail. The case might be argued at great length; but the citation of this one fact may suffice. The activity prompted by physical pain is an activity of one of the most deeply rooted and powerful of the hormic impulses, the impulse of fear.

If the hormic impulse excited by impressions that involve pain-sensation is not in every case the impulse of the fear instinct, then we can interpret the facts only by postulating a specific impulse of avoidance or withdrawal rooted in a correspondingly specific and simple instinct, closely comparable to the instinct to scratch an itching spot.

The case for desire of pleasure as a motive force is less easily disposed of, the problem is more subtle (18).

Let us note first that pleasure is an abstraction, not a concrete entity or situation; it is a feeling qualifying activity. Hence we find that "pleasures" we are alleged to pursue are pleasurable forms of activity. In every case the activity in question is sustained by some impulse or desire of other nature and origin than a pure desire for pleasure, namely, some hormic impulse. Take the simplest instances, most confidently cited by the hedonist—the pleasures of the table and of sex. A man is said to seek the pleasures of the table. What in reality he does is to satisfy his appetite for food, his hormic urge to eat, in the most pleasurable manner, choosing those food-substances which, in the light of past experience, he knows will most effectively stimulate and satisfy this impulse. But without the appetite, the hormic urge, there is no pleasure. So also of the man alleged to pursue the pleasures of sex. Moved or motivated by the sex urge he chooses those ways of indulging it which experience has shown him to be most effective in stimulating and satisfying the urge. But without the hormic urge there is no pleasure to be had.

These instances seem to be typical of all the multitude of cases in which men are said to seek pleasure as their goal. Take the complex case of the man who is said to pursue the pleasure of fame or of power. In pursuit of fame or power many a man shuns delights and lives laborious days. But he is moved, his efforts are sustained, by the desire of fame or power, not by the desire of pleasure. If there were not within him the hormic urge to figure in the eyes of the world or to exert power over others, he could find no pleasure in pursuing and in attaining these goals, and he would not in fact pursue them. You may paint the delights of fame or of power in the most glowing colors to the boy or man who is by nature meek and humble; and your eloquence will fail to stir within him any responsive chord, for in his composition the chord is lacking. On the other hand, in the man in whom the self-assertive impulse is naturally strong, this impulse readily becomes the desire of fame or of power; and, under the driving power of such desire, he may sacrifice all "pleasures," perhaps with full recognition that fame can come only after his death, or that the attainment of power will involve him in most burdensome and exacting responsibilities. Without the hormic urge which sets his goal, neither will he pursue those goals nor would he find any pleasure in the possession of fame or power, if these came to him as a free gift of the gods. These surely are simple truths illustrated by countless instances in fiction and in real life.

Take one more instance. Revenge, it is said, is sweet; and men are said to seek the pleasures of revenge. But, if the injured man is a meek and humble creature, if the injury does not evoke in him a burning desire to humble his adversary, to get even with him, to assert his power over him, the statement that revenge is sweet will have no meaning for him, he will have no impulse to avenge his injury, and the imagining of injury to the adversary will neither afford nor promise him pleasure. On the other hand, injury to the proud self-assertive man provokes in him the vengeful impulse, and in planning his revenge he may well gloat upon the prospect of hurting his adversary; and, if he is a peculiarly sophisticated and ruthless person, he may choose such means to that goal as experience leads him to believe will be most gratifying, most pleasurable.

It is needless to multiply alleged instances of pleasure-seeking; all alike fall under this one formula: the pleasure is not an end in itself; it is incidental to the pursuit and attainment of some goal towards which some hormic impulse sets.

Perhaps a word should be added concerning beauty. Surely, it may be urged, we seek to attain the beautiful and we value the beautiful object for the sake of the pleasure it gives us! Here again hedonist aesthetic inverts the true relations. The foundations of all aesthetic theory

are here in question. It must suffice to say that the beauty
of an object consists not in its power to excite in us a
complex of sensations of pleasurable feeling-tone (if it
were so, a patchwork quilt should be as beautiful as a
Turner landscape); it consists rather in the power of the
object to evoke in us a multitude of conations that work
together in delicately balanced harmony to attain satisfaction in a rich and full appreciation of the significance
of the object.[11]

A second widely accepted supplementation of the
hormic theory is that best represented by the thesis of
Dr. R. S. Woodworth's little book, *Dynamic Psychology*
(32). I have criticized this at length elsewhere (15) and
can therefore deal with it briefly.

Woodworth's thesis may be briefly stated by adopting
the language of the passage cited above from Dr. Drever,
in which he distinguishes between "capacities" for activities, on the one hand, and, on the other, "conscious
impulses, the driving forces to those activities without
which the capacities would be meaningless."

The "capacities" that are inborn become immensely
differentiated and multiplied in the growing child; all
these may be divided roughly into two great classes,

[11] This topic is closely connected with the much neglected
problem of the acquirement of "tastes," a problem I have
dealt with in my *Character and the Conduct of Life* (20).
Since this article was put in print the International Library
of Psychology has published a volume (*Pleasure and Instinct*:
A Study in the Psychology of Human Actions. London & New
York: Harcourt, Brace, 1930.) wholly devoted to the examination of the question discussed in the foregoing section. The
author, A. H. Burlton Allen, after carefully examining the
question from every point of view and in the light of all available evidence arrives at the conclusion that the pure hormic
theory as defined in this article and in my various books is the
only tenable theory of human action. The writer says on p.
273: "Thus it is no doubt true that there is in the feelings no
original force that leads to action. The source of all movement
and action lies in the driving force of the main instincts, that
is to say, in the inherent energy of the organism striving towards outlet in the forms prescribed by its inherited structure.
The feelings of pleasure and unpleasure are secondary results
dependant on the successful or unsuccessful working of these
instincts."

capacities of thinking (of ideation) and capacities of acting, of skilled movement. Now Woodworth's contention is that every such capacity is intrinsically not only a capacity but also a spring of energy, a source of impulsive or motive power; it is implied that every capacity to think or to act in a certain way is also *ipso facto* a tendency to think or to act in that way. To put it concretely —if I have acquired the capacity to recite the alphabet, I have acquired also a tendency to repeat it; if I have acquired the capacity to solve quadratic equations, I have acquired a tendency to solve them; and so on of all the multitude of specific capacities of thinking and acting which all of us acquire.

This is the modern form of the old intellectualistic doctrine that ideas are forces; and its long sway proves that it has its allure, if no solid foundation. The hormic theory contends that there is no truth, or, if any truth, then but the very smallest modicum in this doctrine. It asks: If each one of the immense array of capacities possessed by a man is also intrinsically a tendency to exercise itself, what determines that at any moment only a certain very small number of them come into action? The old answer was given in the theory of the association of ideas. Its defects, its utter inadequacy, have been expounded again and again. Yet it rears its head again in this disguised modern form. The hormic answer to the question is that the "capacities" are but so much latent machinery, functional units of differentiated structure; and that the hormic impulses, working largely through the system of associative links between "capacities," bring into play in turn such capacities as are adapted for service in the pursuit of the natural goals of those impulses. In other words, it maintains that the whole of the machinery of capacities and associative links is dominated by the "interest" of the moment, by conation, by the prevalent desires and active impulses at work in the organism.

It points to "capacities," simple or complex, that remain latent and unused for years, and then, when "the interest" in whose service they were developed is revived, are awakened once more by some change in the man's circumstances, are brought back into action in the service of the renewed interest; as when a man, having become a parent, recites once more for his children the nursery rhymes and the fairy stories he has learned in childhood.

It may be suggested that the current psychoanalytic treatment of the "complex" is in harmony with Woodworth's principle; that in this special case "ideas" or "capacities" are validly treated as possessing, in their own right, motive power or conative energy.

It is true that much of the language of Professor Freud and other psychoanalysts seems to countenance this interpretation of the facts. But it must be remembered that the energy of the complex is regarded as in some sense derived from some instinct, generally the sex instinct; it is *libido*. And though these authors speak of emotionally charged ideas, or ideas *besetzt* with emotional energy (as though each complex owed its power to a charge of libido imparted once for all to it), yet it is, I think, in line with Freud's general treatment to say that such a "complex" is a "capacity," a structural unit, which has acquired such connections with the sex (or other) instinct that the *libido*, or hormic energy of the instinct, readily flows into it and works through it, and thus is determined to modes of expression recognizable as due to the influence of the complex. Consider a fear complex, say a phobia for running water. There has been acquired a peculiar formation which leads to a paroxysm of fear with great expenditure of energy upon the perception of running water, a reaction which may be repeated at long intervals through many years. Are we to suppose that this formation, the complex, contains as an integral part of itself all the energy and all the complex structural organization which every manifestation of fear implies, that each fear complex involves a duplication of the fear organization peculiar to itself? Surely not! The essence of the new formation is such a functional relation between the perceptual system concerned in the recognition of running water and the whole apparatus of fear, that the perception becomes one of the various afferent channels through which the fear system may be excited. In this connection it is to be remembered that a sufficient mass of evidence points to the thalamic region as the principal seat of the great affective systems or centers of instinctive excitement. In neurological terms, the perception of running water is in the main a cortical event, while the manifestation of fear is in the main a subcortical or thalamic event; and the essential neural ground of the complex manifestation is a special, acquired corticothalamic connection between the two events, or, more strictly, between the two neuron systems concerned in the two events and respectively located in cortex and in thalamus.

The hormist can find no clear instances that support Woodworth's thesis and can point to a multitude of instances which indicate an absence of all driving power in the "capacities" as such. He maintains therefore that the burden of proof lies upon his opponents; and, though he cannot conclusively prove the negative thesis, that no "capacity" has driving power, he sees no ground for accepting this supplement to the hormic theory.

There remain for brief consideration two very modern theories which claim to find the hormic theory in need of supplementation and to supply such supplement.

I refer first to the psychology of Dr. Ludwig Klages and of his able disciple, Dr. Hans Prinzhorn.[12] According to this teaching (I write subject to correction, for it is not easy to grasp), the hormic theory is true of the life of animals and of the lower functions of the human organism, of all the life of instinct and perceptual activity; but the life of man is complicated by the cooperation of two factors of a different order, *Geist* and *Wille*, spirit and will, two aspects of a higher purely spiritual principle which is not only of an order different from that of the hormic impulses but is in many respects antagonistic to them, a disturbing influence that threatens to pervert and even destroy the instinctive basis of human life.

I know not what to say of this doctrine. To me it seems to involve a radical dualism not easily to be accepted. It seems to contain echoes of old ways of thinking, of the old opposition of the instinct of animals to

[12] Set forth in numerous works of which one only, Klages' *Psychology of Character* (10) has been translated into English. Prinzhorn's *Leib-seele Einheit* (28) gives the best brief approach to this system.

the reason of man, of Hegel's objectified spirit, even of
Descartes' dualism, the animal body a machine complicated in man by the intervention of reason, although,
it is true, these authors repudiate whole-heartedly the
mechanical physiology. I suggest that the *Geist* and *Wille*
which, as these authors rightly insist, make human life so
widely different from the life of even the highest animals,
are to be regarded not as some mysterious principles of a
radically different order from any displayed in animal
life; that they are rather to be identified with what the
Germans call *objective Geist*, objectified spirit of humanity, the system of intellectual process and of cultural
values which has been slowly built up as the traditional
possession of each civilization and largely fixed in the
material forms of art and science, in architecture, in tools,
in written and printed words, in enduring institutions of
many kinds. Each human being absorbs from his social
environment some large part of this objectified spirit; and
it is this, working within him, that gives rise to the
higher manifestations of human life which in Klages' doctrine are ascribed to *Geist* and *Wille*. Until this interpretation of the facts shall have been shown to be inadequate, there would seem to be no sufficient foundation
for the new dualism of Klages and Prinzhorn.

Lastly, I mention an interesting supplement to the
hormic theory offered in a recent book by Mr. Olaf
Stapledon (30). The author begins by accepting the
hormic theory in a thoroughgoing teleological sense. But
he goes on to say: "A human being's inheritance would
seem to include a capacity for discovering and conating
tendencies beyond the inherited nature of his own organism, or his own biological needs." And he chooses, as
the clearest illustrations of what he means, instances of
love of one person for another. Criticizing my view that
in sex love we have a sentiment in which the principal
motive powers are the impulses of the sexual and of the
parental instincts in reciprocal interplay, he writes: "But
this theory ignores an important difference between
parental behavior and love, and between the tender emotions and love. Parents do, as a matter of fact, often love
their children; but they do also often merely behave
parentally toward them, and feel tender emotion toward

them. The love of a parent for a child may be said to be 'derived' from the parental tendency, in the sense that this tendency first directed attention to the child, and made possible the subsequent *discovery of the child* as itself a living centre of tendencies. And it may well be that in all love there is something of this instinctive parental behaviour. But genuine love, for whatever kind of object, is very different from the tender emotion and from all strictly instinctive parental behaviour. . . . Genuine love . . . entails the espousal of the other's needs in the same direct manner in which one espouses one's own private needs. . . . Merely instinctive behaviour is, so to speak, the conation of a tendency or complex of tendencies of the agent's own body or person. Genuine love is the conation of tendencies of another person . . . if love occurs, or in so far as it occurs, the other is regarded, not as a stimulus, but as a centre of tendencies demanding conation in their own right."

Referring to the patriotic sentiment of Joan of Arc, Stapledon writes: "That sentiment certainly did become the ruling factor of her life. And, further, whatever its instinctive sources, her cognition of her social environment turned it into something essentially different from any mere blend of instinctive impulses. The chief weakness of instinct psychology is that it fails, in spite of all efforts to the contrary, to do justice to the part played in behaviour by environment. And this failure is most obvious in human behaviour." He adds that the "instinct psychologists . . . have left out the really distinctive feature of human behaviour."

What, then, is this distinctive feature? Here is a new challenge to the hormic theory; a denial not of its truth, up to a certain point, but of its adequacy to cover all the facts and especially the facts of distinctively human activity.

The "distinctive feature," this alleged source of conations not derived from native impulses, is defined as follows: "I am suggesting, then, that the essential basis of conation is not that some tendency of the organism, or of a simple inherited mental structure, is the source (direct or indirect) of every conative act, but that *every* cognition of tendency *may* give rise to a conative act. Every tendency which is an element in the mental content suggests a conation, and is the ground of at least incipient conation. If the tendency does not conflict with other and well-established conative ends, its fulfilment will be desired."

Now, obviously, if this doctrine be true, it is very important. For among tendencies the cognition of any one of which gives rise to corresponding conation, the desire of its fulfilment, Mr. Stapledon includes not only all human and animal tendencies, but also all physical tendencies, e.g., the tendency of a stream of water to run downhill, of a stone to fall to the ground, of a needle to fly to the magnet. Of every tendency he asserts: "In the mere act of apprehending *it*, we desire its fulfilment." And "if we ask—'How does the primitive self expand into the developed self?' we find the answer is that the most important way of expanding is by the cognition of a wider field of objective tendencies and the conative espousal of those tendencies"; for "any objective tendency may enter the mental content and influence the will in its own right."

I find this theory very intriguing. But I find also the grounds advanced as its foundation quite unconvincing. They are two: first, the alleged inadequacy of the instinct theory; secondly, the assertion that every cognition of any tendency tends to evoke corresponding or congruent conation. As regards the former ground, I am, no doubt, a prejudiced witness, yet, in Stapledon's chosen instance of love, I cannot admit the inadequacy. I admit that Joan of Arc's patriotic behavior was "different from any mere blend of instinctive impulses." Here Stapledon has failed, I think, to grasp the implication of the theory of the sentiments. In the working of a developed sentiment, whether love of country, love of parent for child, or of man for woman, we have to do not merely with a blending and conflicting of primitive impulses. Such a sentiment is a most complex organization comprising much elaborated cognitive structure as well as instinctive dispositions, and its working can only properly be viewed in the light of the principles of emergence and Gestalt.

Further, Stapledon seems to neglect to take account of the principles of passive and of active sympathy. It is true, I think, that the cognition of a tendency at work in another person tends to evoke or bring into activity the corresponding tendency in the observer; and in very sympathetic personalities this sympathetic induction works strongly and frequently. When we recognize fully these facts, we cover, I suggest, the manifestation of such complex sentiments as love, which Stapledon chooses to illustrate the inadequacy of the hormic principles. As to his essential novelty, his claim that cognition of any tendency, even merely physical tendency, gives rise to conation similarly directed, I remain entirely unconvinced. There are two parts of this thesis, the second depending on the former; and both seem to me highly questionable. First, he assumes that the conation rooted in the instinctive nature arises through cognition of an active tendency at work in oneself. This is to make a two- or three-stage affair of the simplest impulsive action. First, the tendency is aroused into activity, presumably by cognition of some object or situation; secondly, it is cognized; thirdly, this cognition gives rise to conation. Is not this pure mythology? Is it correct to say that we strive only when we "espouse" a tendency which we cognize as at work within us? Is it not rather true that the activity of the tendency primarily aroused by cognition of some object or situation is the conation which proceeds under guidance of further cognition. It seems clear that the instinctive impulse may and often does work subconsciously, that is, without being cognized; and in any case, its working is so obscure to cognition that the majority of psychologists, failing to cognize or recognize it in any form, deny the reality of such experience of active tendency.

Admitting the wide range in human life of the sympathetic principle, admitting that, in virtue of this principle, cognition of desire in others evokes similar desire in ourselves, or a tendency towards the same goal, or a tendency to cooperate with or promote the striving cognized in the other, I cannot find sufficient ground for believing that cognition of tendency in physical objects also directly evokes in us congruent tendency or conation. I would maintain that only when in the mood of poetry or primitive animism we personify natural objects and events, only then do we feel sympathy, or antagonism;

and on the whole we are as liable to feel antagonism as sympathy. When I contemplate the flow of a river I murmur with the poet, "Even the weariest river winds somewhere safe to sea," and may feel a sympathetic inclination to glide with the current; but I may equally well (especially if a resident of the lower Mississippi valley) regard the flowing river as a hostile force against which I incline to struggle, or (if I am a thrifty Scot) as a distressing waste of energy; and, if it is a mountain stream, I may even be moved to try to dam its course. Immersed in the water, I am equally ready to enjoy swimming with the current or struggling up-stream, letting myself be rushed along with the breaker or hurling myself against it. If I contemplate the wind gently moving the branches of a tree or caressing my face, I may feel it to be a friendly power and exclaim, "O Wild West Wind, thou breath of autumn's being"; or I may observe with delight the little breezes that "dusk and shiver." But if I apprehend the wind as tearing at a tree, buffeting the ship, or lashing the waves to fury, I am all against it as a fierce and cruel power to be fought and withstood; I sympathize with the straining tree, the laboring ship, or the rock or stout building that stands foursquare to all the winds that blow. In short, my reaction to the wind varies as it seems to whisper, to whistle, to sing, to murmur, to sigh, to moan, to roar, to bluster, to shriek, to rage, to tear, to storm. Such sympathies and antagonisms provoked by the forces of nature are the very breath of nature poetry; but they seem to me to afford no support to Mr. Stapledon's thesis. The primitive animistic tendency is, I submit, an extension of primitive or passive sympathy; an imaginative extension to inanimate nature of the emotional stirrings we directly or intuitively discern in our fellow-creatures, rather than an immediate and fundamental reaction to all cognition of physical agency, as Mr. Stapledon maintains. In gentle, highly sympathetic natures, such as Wordsworth's, it works chiefly in the form of sympathy with natural forces; but more pugnacious and self-assertive natures are more readily stirred to antagonism and opposition than to congruent conation. It would seem that, as is commonly the case when writers on ethics undertake to construct their own psychology, Stapledon's supplementation of the hormic psychology is determined by the needs of his ethical theory rather than by consideration of the observable facts of experience and activity.

I conclude, then, that the hormic theory is adequate and requires no such supplementations as those examined in this section and found to be ill-based and otiose.

THE ADVANTAGES OF THE HORMIC THEORY

One advantage of the hormic theory over all others is that it enables us to sketch in outline an intelligible, consistent, and tenable story of continuous organic evolution, evolution of bodily forms and mental functions in intelligible relation to one another; and this is something which no other theory can achieve. It does not attempt the impossible task of describing the genesis of experience out of the purely physical and of teleological activity out of purely mechanistic events. It does not make the illegitimate assumption that experience can be analyzed into and regarded as compounded out of simple particles or entities. It insists that experience, or each phase of it, is always a unitary whole having aspects that are distinguishable but not separable. It finds good reason to believe that the life of the simplest creature involves such experience, however utterly vague and undifferentiated it may be. It regards the story of organic evolution as one of progressive differentiation and specialization of structure, of experience and of activity from the most rudimentary and simplest forms. It regards the striving capacities, the hormic tendencies, of each species as having been differentiated out of a primal urge to live, to be active, to seek, to assimilate, to build up, to energize, to counteract the forces of dissolution. Such differentiations of striving involve parallel differentiations of the cognitive function subserving the discrimination of goals. And still further differentiation of it for the discernment and adaptation of means results in longer and more varied chains of activity through which remoter and more difficult goals are attained. The theory recognizes that only in the human species does cognitive differentiation attain such a level that detailed foresight of remote goals

becomes possible, with such definite hormic fixation on
the goal as characterizes action properly called purposive
in the fullest sense of the word. But it claims that,
though the foresight of even the higher animals is but of
short range, envisaging only the result to be attained by
the next step of action, and that perhaps very vaguely,
the cognitive dispositions of the animal are often linked
in such fashion as to lead on the hormic urge from step
to step, until finally the biological goal is attained and
the train of action terminates in satisfaction. It finds in
human activity and experience parallels to all the simpler
forms of activity displayed and of experience implied in
the animals. It sees in the growing infant signs of development from almost blind striving with very short-range
and vague foresight (when its cognitive powers are still
but slightly differentiated) to increasingly long-range and
more adequate foresight enriched by the growing wealth
and variety of memory. It insists that memory is for the
sake of foresight, and foresight for the sake of action;
and that neither can be validly conceived other than as
the working of a forward urge that seeks always something more behind and beyond that which is given in
sense presentation, a something more that will satisfy
the hormic urge and bring it for the time being to rest,
or permit it to be turned by new sense impressions to
some new goal.

If we turn from the descriptive account of evolution
to the problem of the dynamics of the process, the
hormic theory again is the only one that can offer an intelligible and self-consistent scheme. It notes how the
human creature, through constant striving with infinitely
varied circumstances, carries the differentiation of both
cognitive and striving powers far beyond the point to
which the hereditary momentum will carry them, the
point common to the species, how it develops new dis-
criminations, modified goals of appetition and aversion,
modified trains of activity for pursuit or retreat. It notes
that these modifications are achieved under the guidance
of the pleasure and the pain, the satisfaction and dissatisfaction, that attend success and failure respectively; it
inclines to view the evolution or rather the epigenesis of
the individual creature's adaptations as the model in the

light of which we may interpret the epigenesis of racial adaptations. Such interpretation implies acceptance of Lamarckian transmission; but, since the only serious ground for rejecting this is the assumption that mechanistic categories are sufficient in biology, an assumption which the hormic psychology rejects, this implication is in its eyes no objection. Rather it points to the increasing weight of evidence of the reality of Lamarckian transmission.[13]

The hormic theory insists that the differentiation of instinctive tendencies has been, throughout the scale of animal evolution, the primary or leading feature of each step. Bodily organs cannot be supposed to have acquired new forms and functional capacities that remained functionless until some congruent variation of instinctive tendency brought them into play. Rather, it is necessary to believe that, in the case of every new development of form or function, the first step was the variation of the instinctive nature of the species toward such activities as required for their efficient exercise the peculiarities of form and function in question. Given such variation, we can understand how natural selection may have brought about the development in the species of the peculiarities of bodily form and function best suited to subserve such modified or new instinctive tendency. Thus the theory overcomes the greatest difficulty of the neo-Darwinian theory, the difficulty, namely, that, if novelties of form and function are to be established in a species, very many of the members must have varied in the same direction at the same time and in such a wide degree as will give survival value to the variation. For, given some changed environmental conditions of a species (e.g., a growing scarcity of animal food for the carnivorous land ancestor of the seal), the intelligence common to all members might well lead all of them to pursue prey by a

[13] Since 1920 I have conducted an experiment on strictly Lamarckian principles and have found clear-cut evidence of increasing facility in successive generations of animals trained to execute a particular task. This very great increase of facility seems explicable in no other way than by transmission of the modifications acquired by the efforts of the individuals. Cf. two reports in the *British Journal of Psychology* (19, 22).

new method (the method of swimming and diving). And if this relatively new mode of behavior became fixed, if the tendency to adopt it became stronger through repeated successful efforts to secure prey in this fashion, natural selection might well perpetuate all congruent bodily variations and might eliminate variations of an opposite kind; and thus convert the legs of the species into flippers. This is the principle that has been named "organic selection," rendered effective by the recognition of the causal efficacy of hormic striving and the reality of Lamarckian transmission, a principle which without such recognition remains of very dubious value.[14]

The hormic theory thus renders possible a workable theory of animal evolution, one under which the mind, or the mental function of cognition-conation, is the growing point of the organism and of the species, a theory under which the intelligent striving of the organism is the creative activity to which evolution is due. Surely such a theory is more acceptable than any that pretends to illuminate the mystery of evolution by such utterly vague terms as "orthogenesis" or "*élan vital*" or "the momentum of life."

The hormic theory is radically opposed to intellectualism and all its errors, the errors that have been the chief bane of psychology (and of European culture in general) all down the ages. It does not set out with some analytic description of purely cognitive experience, and then find itself at a loss for any intelligible functional relation between this and bodily activities. It recognizes fully the conative nature of all activity and regards the cognitive power as everywhere the servant and the guide of striving. Thus it is fundamentally dynamic and leads to a psychology well adapted for application to the sciences and practical problems of human life, those of education, of hygiene, of therapy, of social activity, of religion, of mythology, of aesthetics, of economics, of politics and the rest.[15]

[14] As formulated many years ago by the neo-Darwinians, E. B. Poutton, J. M. Baldwin, and Lloyd Morgan.

[15] When a young man I was invited to dine with a distinguished economist and a leading psychologist of that period. It was mentioned that I was taking up psychology. "Ah!" said

Of all forms of psychology the hormic is the only one that can give to philosophy the psychological basis essential to it. Philosophy is properly concerned with values, with evaluation and with standards and scales of value; it seeks to establish the relative values of the goals men seek, of their ideals, of the forms of character and types of conduct. All such valuation is relative to human nature; a scale of values formulated with reference, not to man as he is or may be, but to some creature of radically different constitution would obviously be of little value to men; and philosophy can advance towards a true scale of values only in proportion as it founds itself upon a true account of human nature, its realities and its potentialities. The claim, then, that hormic psychology is the psychology needed by philosophy may seem merely a repetition of the claim that it is true. But it is more than this; for a glance at the history of philosophy shows that the hormic psychology is the only one with which philosophy can work, the only one on which it can establish a scale of values, that does not break to pieces under the slightest examination.

The intellectualist philosophy, adopting an intellectualist psychology of ideas, finds its source and criterion of all values in logical consistency of its system; and surely it is plain that men do not and will not bear the ills they have, still less struggle heroically against them, supported only by the satisfaction of knowing themselves to be part of a perfectly logical system.

The mechanistic psychology can recognize no values; can give no account of the process of valuation. At the best it can but (as in Mr. B. Russell's essay, "A Free Man's Worship") hurl defiance at a universe without meaning and without value which man is powerless to alter.

The hedonist psychology consorts only with a hedonist

---

the economist, "Psychology! Yes, very important, very important! Association of ideas and all that sort of thing. What!" It was obvious to me that he did not attach the slightest importance to psychology and had neither the faintest inkling of any bearing of it on economics, nor any intention of seeking any such relation. From that moment dates my revulsion against the traditional intellectualistic psychology.

philosophy, which can save itself from being a philosophy of the pig-trough only by postulating with J. S. Mill, in defiance of clarity and of logic, a profound difference of value between higher and lower pleasures.

The hormic psychology alone offers an intelligible and consistent account of human valuations and at the same time offers to philosophy a scientific foundation in which freedom of the rational will of man, the power of creating real novelties, actual and ideal, and the power of self-development towards the ideal both of the individual and of the race, can find their proper place consistently with its fundamental postulates. It is thus the only foundation for a philosophy of meliorism.

The hormic theory, holding fast to the fact that cognition and conation are inseparable aspects of all mental life, does not elaborate a scheme of the cognitive life, a plan of the structure and functioning of the intellect, and leave to some other discipline (be it called ethology or praxiology or ethics) the task of giving some account of character. For it understands that intellect and character are, as structures, just as inseparable as the functions of cognition and conation, are but two aspects, distinguishable only in abstraction, of the structure of personality.

Recognizing that introspection can seize and fix in verbal report only the elaborated outcome of a vast and complex interplay of psychophysical events, it avoids the common error of setting over against one another two minds, or two parts of one mind or personality, under such heads as "the Conscious" and "the Unconscious," and steadily sets its face against this mystification, which, though it appeals so strongly to the popular taste for the mysterious and the bizarre, is profoundly misleading.

It recognizes that the fundamental nature of the hormic impulse is to work towards its natural goal and to terminate or cease to operate only when and in so far as its natural goal is attained; that the impulse which, in the absence of conflicting impulses, works toward its goal in trains, long or short, of conscious activity (activity, that is, which we can introspectively observe and report with very various degrees of clearness and adequacy) is apt to be driven from the field of conscious activity by conflicting impulses; that, when thus driven from the conscious field, it is not necessarily (perhaps not in any instance) arrested, terminated, brought to zero; that, rather, any impulse, if it is driven from the conscious field before its goal is attained, continues to work subterraneously, subconsciously, and, so working, may obtain partial expressions in the conscious field and in action, expressions which often take the form of not easily interpretable distortions of conscious thinking and of bodily action; that such subconscious activity (but presumably not in any strict sense unconscious activity, far removed though it be from the possibility of introspective observation and report) is a normal feature of the complex life of man, in whom so many natural impulses are checked and repressed by those evoked through the demands of society; that in this way we are to interpret the phenomena now attracting the attention of experimental psychologists under the heads of "perseveration" and "secondary function," as well as all the many morbid and quasi-morbid phenomena of dream life, hallucinations, delusions, compulsions, obsessions, and all the multitudinous bodily and mental symptoms of functional disorder.

The principles of the hormic theory are capable of extension downwards from the conscious life of man, not only to the more explicitly teleological actions of animals, but also to the problems of physiology, the problems of the regulation and interaction of the functioning of all the tissues. It is thus the truly physiological psychology, the psychology that can assimilate and apply the findings of physiology, and in turn can illuminate the problems of physiology, and thus lead to a comprehensive science of the organism; a science which will not regard the organism as a machine with conscious processes somehow mysteriously tacked on to it as "epiphenomena," but a science which will regard the organism as a true organic unity all parts of which are in reciprocal interplay with all other parts and with the whole; a whole which is not merely the sum of the parts, but a synthetic unity maintained by the systematic reciprocal interaction of all the parts, a unity of integration, a colonial system of lesser units, whose unity is maintained by the harmonious hormic activity of its members in due subordination to the whole.

The hormic psychology has the advantage that it does not pretend to know the answers to the great unsolved riddles of the universe. It leaves to the future the solution of such problems as the relation of the organic to the inorganic realm, the origin or advent of life in our world, the place and destiny of the individual and of the race in the universe, the possibility of powers and potentialities of the race not yet recognized by science. In short, it does not assume any particular cosmology; it recognizes the littleness of man's present understanding; it makes for the open mind and stimulates the spirit of inquiry, and is hospitable to all empirical evidences and all legitimate speculations.[16]

It is impossible to set forth here the many advantages of the theory in its detailed application to all the special problems of psychology. It must suffice to point out that, unlike the psychologies which begin by accepting such artificial entities of abstraction as reflexes,[17] sensations, ideas, concepts, feelings, in mechanistic interplay according to laws of association, fusion, reproduction, and what-not, it regards all experience as expressive of a total activity that is everywhere hormic, selective, teleological. Thus its recognition of the selective goal-seeking nature of our activity, of all the facts implied by the words

[16] Hence it does not close the mind to the much disputed field of alleged phenomena investigated by the Societies for Psychical Research, but makes for a truly scientific attitude towards them, an attitude so conspicuous by its absence in most men of science and especially in academic psychologists.

[17] It is of interest to note that from the purely physiological side protests against the mechanical atomizing tendency multiply apace. One of the latest and most important of these is a paper read before the International Congress of Psychology in September, 1929, by Dr. G. E. Coghill, who showed good embryological grounds for refusing to regard the spinal reflexes as functional units that first take shape independently and later are brought into some kind of relation with one another. He showed reason to believe that each reflex unit develops by differentiation within the total nervous system of which it never ceases to be a functional part in reciprocal influence with all other parts.

"desire," "motivation," "attention," and "will," is not reluctant, grudging, and inadequate, added under compulsion of the facts to a mechanical system into which they refuse to fit. It recognizes these aspects as fundamental, and traces the genesis of desire, attention, and rational volition from their germs in the hormic impulses of primitive organisms.

The hormic theory projects a completely systematic and self-consistent psychology on the basis of its recognition of the whole of the organized mind of the adult as a structure elaborated in the service of the hormic urge to more and fuller life. Every part of this vastly complex structure it regards as serving to differentiate the hormic impulses, and to direct them with ever increasing efficiency towards their natural goals in a world of infinite complexity that offers a multitude of possible routes to any goal, possibilities among which the organism chooses wisely according to the richness of its apparatus of sensory apprehension and its span of synthetic integration of many relations, the effective organization of its memory, the nicety of its discriminatory judgments, and its sagacity in seizing, out of a multitude of possibilities offered by sense-presentation and memory, the possibilities most relevant to its purposes.

Especially clearly appears the advantage of the hormic psychology in that it is able to render intelligible account of the organization of the affective or emotional-conative side of the mental structure, a relatively independent part or aspect of the whole of vast importance which remains a closed book to all psychologies of the intellectualistic mechanistic types. This side of the mental structure, which the latter psychologies ignore or recognize most inadequately with such words as "attitudes" and "sets," is treated a little less cavalierly by the psychoanalytic school under the all-inclusive term—"the Unconscious," and a little more analytically under the heads of "complexes" and "emotionally toned ideas." But the treatment remains very confused and inadequate, confining itself almost exclusively to the manifestations of conflict and disorder in this part of the mind. The hormic psychology, on the other hand, insists that the elucidation of this part of the mental organization is theoretically no less important, and practically far more important, than that of the intellectual structure and functions, and is an integral part of the task of psychology, not a task to be handed over to some other science, be it called ethics, or characterology, or ethology, or praxiology, or by any other name; for it insists that we cannot understand the intellectual processes without some comprehension of the organization and working of the affective processes whose servants they are.

Towards the elucidation of this part of the problem of psychology it offers the doctrine of the sentiments, the true functional systems of the developed mind, through the development of which in the growing individual the native hormic impulses become further differentiated and directed to a multitude of new and specialized goals, a process which obscurely and profoundly modifies the nature of these native tendencies; for in these new and individually acquired systems, the sentiments, the native tendencies are brought into various cooperations, form new dynamic syntheses in which their individuality is lost and from which true novelties of desire, of emotion, and of action emerge.

Further, it aims to show how these fundamental functional systems, the sentiments, tend to become organized in one comprehensive system, character, which, when it is harmoniously integrated, can override all the crude promptings of instinctive impulse however strong, can repress, redirect, or sublimate them on every occasion, and thus, in intimate cooperation with the intellectual organization, engender that highest manifestation of personality, rational volition.

Lastly, the hormic theory is ready to welcome and is capable of assimilating all that is sound and useful in the newer schools of psychology. Unlike the various psychologies currently taught in the American colleges, it does not find itself indifferent or positively hostile to these newer movements because incapable of assimilating what is of value in them. Rather it finds something of truth and value in the rival psychoanalytic doctrines of Freud, of Jung, and of Adler, in the allied doctrines of Gestalt and Emergence, in the *verstehende* psychology of the *Geisteswissenschaftler*, in the teachings of Spranger, of Erismann, of Jaspers, in the *personalistische* psychology of Stern, in the *Charackterologie* of Klages and Prinzhorn, in the child studies of the Bühlers, in the correlational studies and conclusions of Spearman, and in the quite peculiar system of dynamic interpretation which Dr. Kurt Lewin is developing. This catholicity, this power of comprehensive assimilation of new truth from widely differing systems of psychological thinking is, perhaps, the best proof of the fundamental rightness of the hormic psychology.

ORIGINS OF THE HORMIC PSYCHOLOGY

The psychology of Aristotle is thoroughly teleological; but it can hardly be claimed that it was purely hormic. In his time the distinction between mechanistic and teleological explanations and that between hedonist and hormic explanations had not been sharply defined. As with most of the later authors who approximate a hormic psychology, his hormic theory is infected with hedonism.[18] But it may at least be said that in Greek thought there were already established two broadly contrasting views of the world, the Apollinian and the Dionysian, and that Aristotle was on the Dionysian side.[19]

The Apollinian view was the parent of European in-

[18] Professor W. A. Hammond summarizes Aristotle's theory of action as follows: "Desire, as Aristotle employs it, is not a purely pathic or effective element. Feeling as such (theoretically) is completely passive—mere enjoyment of the pleasant or mere suffering of the painful. Aristotle, however, describes desire as an effort towards the attainment of the pleasant; i.e., he includes in it an activity or a conative element. It is feeling with an added quality of impulse (*Trieb*)." Here we see the cloven hoof of hedonism. The hormic theory would say rather that desire is impulse (*Trieb*) with an added quality of feeling.

[19] Nietzsche seems to have been the first to point clearly to these contrasting and rival world-views. I have attempted elsewhere (23) to show how these two currents have been represented in psychology all down the stream of European thought and how the distinction affords the best clue to a useful classification of psychological theories, since it distinguishes them in respect to their most fundamental features, their inclination towards intellectualism or towards voluntarism.

tellectualism, of which the keynote has been Socrates'
identification of virtue with knowledge. It has generated
the allied, though superficially so different, systems of
absolute idealism and of Newtonian mechanism; and
modern psychology, from Descartes and Locke onward,
has reflected in the main the influence of these two
systems, with their fundamental postulates of the idea
and the atom (or mass-point) in motion.

The inadequacy of the Apollinian view, the misleading nature of its ideal of perfect intelligibility, of complete explanation of all events by deduction from first
principles or transparent postulates, has now been manifested in the collapse of pure idealism and of the strictly
mechanistic physics; and no less clearly in the culmina-
tion of centuries of effort to reconcile the Apollinian
ideal with the facts of nature in the doctrine of psychophysical parallelism; a doctrine so unsatisfactory, so obviously a makeshift, so unintelligible, so obstructive to
all deeper understanding of nature, that although it was,
in one form or another, very widely accepted at the close
of the nineteenth century, the century dominated by the
Apollinian tradition, it has now been almost universally
abandoned, even by those who have nothing to put in its
place.

The Dionysian tradition has lived in the main outside
the academies. European thought, though it was dominated by Aristotle until the end of the mediaeval period,
was more concerned with reason than with action, and
yielded more and more to Apollinian tradition; and,
with the triumph of intellectualism at and after the
Renaissance, the Dionysian tradition was represented
only by the poets and came near to exclusion from their
pages also in the great age of Reason, the eighteenth
century. The early years of the nineteenth century saw
its revival in the works of the nature poets and of such
philosophers as Oken, Schelling, and Fichte. And in the
Scottish school of mental philosophy it began to find
definite expression in psychology, especially in the works
of Hutcheson and Dugald Stewart, a movement which
was well nigh extinguished by Bain's capitulation to the
intellectualism of the English association school.

On the continent of Europe, Schopenhauer revived it

with his doctrine of the primacy of will; and Von Hartmann, his disciple, may be said to have first written psychology on a purely hormic basis,[20] but marred by the extravagance of his speculations on the unconscious. Nietzsche's scattered contributions to psychology are thoroughly hormic; and Bergson's vague doctrine of the "*élan vital*" can be classed only under the same heading. Freud's psychology would be thoroughly hormic, if he had not spoilt it in his earlier writings by his inclusion of the hedonist fallacy in the shape of his "pleasure principle." My *Introduction to Social Psychology* (13) was, so far as I have learned, the first attempt to construct a foundation for psychology in strict accordance with the hormic principle; and my two *Outlines* (16, 17) represent the first attempt to sketch a complete psychology (normal and abnormal) built on the hormic foundation. It was unfortunate for the hormic theory that my *Social Psychology* was shortly followed by my *Body and Mind* (14). For my defense of animism in that book created in many minds the impression that hormism stands or falls with animism; an impression that has been, I judge, largely responsible for the waning of the influence of the former book in American academic psychology. But the two theories do not necessarily hang together, as is clearly shown by Sir P. T. Nunn, that wisest of professors of education, distinguished as mathematician, philosopher, and psychologist, who founds his educational theory on a thoroughly hormic psychology, while repudiating animism. In his *Education, its Data and First Principles* (26), he has given the most lucid and persuasive statement of the hormic principles. In this statement he makes what is, I believe, the first definite proposal to use the terms *horme* and *hormic* in the sense in which they are used in this essay.

It is fitting, then, that this essay should conclude with citations from Dr. Nunn's book, citations that may serve further to clarify and fix the meaning of the terms *horme* and *hormic* and the implications of the theory.

"We need a name," writes Dr. Nunn, "for the fundamental property expressed in the incessant adjustments and adventures that make up the tissue of life. We are

[20] Cf. his *Die Moderne Psychologie* (4).

directly aware of that property in our conscious activities as an element of "drive," "urge," or felt tendency towards an end. Psychologists call it *conation* and give the name *conative process* to any train of conscious activity which is dominated by such a drive and receives from it the character of unity in diversity." Referring then to instances of the many subconscious activities that find expression in action, he writes: "None of these purposive processes may be called conative, for they lie below, and even far below, the conscious level; yet a super-human spectator, who could watch our mental behavior in the same direct way as we can observe physical events, would see them all as instances of the same class, variant in detail but alike (as we have said) in general plan. In other words, he would see that they all differ from purely mechanical processes by the presence of an internal "drive," and differ from one another only in the material in which the drive works and the character of the ends towards which it is directed. To this element of drive or urge, whether it occurs in the conscious life of man and the higher animals, or in the unconscious activities of their bodies and the (presumably) unconscious behavior of lower animals, we propose to give a single name— horme (ὅρμη). In accordance with this proposal all the purposive processes of the organism are hormic processes, conative processes being the subclass whose members have the special mark of being conscious . . . Horme . . . is the basis of the activities that differentiate the living animal from dead matter, and, therefore, of what we have described as the animal's characteristic attitude of independence towards its world."

Accepting this admirable statement, I will add only one comment. In my recent *Modern Materialism and Emergent Evolution* (21), I have argued that we can interpret the subconscious hormic processes (which Dr. Nunn agrees to regard as purposive or teleological), we can begin to gain some understanding of them, however vague, only if we regard them not as entirely blind but rather as involving, however dimly, something of that foresight (however vague and short-ranging) which is of the essence of our most clearly purposive activities; that therefore we must regard every hormic process as of the

same fundamental nature as our mental activity, even if
that interpretation involves us in a provisional dualism,
held as a working hypothesis the final verdict upon which
can come only with the progress of both the biological
and the physical sciences.

REFERENCES

1. CARR, H. A. *Psychology.* New York: Longmans, Green,
   1925. Pp. 226.
2. DREVER, J. *Instinct in Man.* Cambridge: Cambridge Univ.
   Press, 1917. Pp. x+293.
3. HALDANE, J. S. *The Sciences and Philosophy.* London:
   Hodder, 1929. Pp. 344.
4. HARTMANN, E. v. *Die moderne Psychologie.* Leipzig:
   Haacke, 1901. Pp. vii+474.
5. HERRICK, C. J. The natural history of purpose. *Psychol.
   Rev.,* 1925, 32, 417-430.
6. ———. Biological determinism and human freedom. *Int.
   J. Ethics,* 1926, 37, 36-52.
7. ———. Behavior and mechanism. *Soc. Forces,* 1928, 7,
   1-11.
8. HINGSTON, R. W. G. *Problems of Instinct and Intelligence.*
   London: Arnold, 1928. Pp. viii+296.
9. JENNINGS, H. S. Diverse doctrines of evolution, their relation to the practice of science and of life. *Science,* 1927,
   65, 19-25.
10. KLAGES, L. *The Science of Character.* (Trans. by W. H.
    Johnson.) London: Allen & Unwin, 1929. Pp. 308.
11. LILLIE, R. S. The nature of the vitalistic dilemma. *J. Phil.,*
    1926, 23, 673-682.
12. LODGE, O. Beyond physics. *J. Phil. Stud.,* 1929, 4, 516-546.
13. McDOUGALL, W. *An Introduction to Social Psychology.*
    London: Methuen, 1908. Pp. x+355.
14. ———. *Body and Mind.* New York: Macmillan; London:
    Methuen, 1911. Pp. xix+384.
15. ———. Motives in the light of recent discussion. *Mind,*
    1920, 29, 277-293.
16. ———. *Outline of Psychology.* New York: Scribner's,
    1923. Pp. xvi+456.
17. ———. *Outline of Abnormal Psychology.* New York:
    Scribner's, 1926. Pp. xiii+566.
18. ———. Pleasure, pain and conation. *Brit. J. Psychol.,*
    1926, 17, 171-180.
19. ———. An experiment for the testing of the hypothesis
    of Lamarck. *Brit. J. Psychol.,* 1927, 17, 267-304.

20. ———. *Character and the Conduct of Life*. London: Methuen, 1927. Pp. xiii+287.
21. ———. *Modern Materialism and Emergent Evolution*. New York: Van Nostrand, 1929. Pp. viii+249.
22. ———. Second report on a Lamarckian experiment. *Brit. J. Psychol.*, *J. Phil. Stud.*, 1930, 4, No. 17.
23. ———. The present chaos in psychology and the way out. *J. Phil. Stud.*
24. Morgan, C. L. *Emergent Evolution*. London: Williams & Norgate, 1923. Pp. xii+313.
25. ———. *Life, Mind, and Spirit*. London: Williams & Norgate, 1926. Pp. 356.
26. Nunn, P. T. *Education, its Data and First Principles*. London: Arnold, 1920. Pp. 224.
27. Prince, M. Three fundamental errors of the behaviorists and the reconciliation of the purposive and mechanistic concepts. Chap. 9 in Psychologies of 1925. Worcester, Mass.: Clark Univ. Press, 1926. Pp. 199-220.
28. Prinzhorn, H. *Leib-seele Einheit*. Potsdam: Müller & Kripenhauer, 1927. Pp. 201.
29. Russell, E. S. *The Study of Living Things*. London: Methuen, 1924. Pp. 294.
30. Stapledon, W. O. *A Modern Theory of Ethics: A Study of the Relations of Ethics and Psychology*. London: Methuen, 1929. Pp. 278.
31. Troland, L. T. *The Fundamentals of Human Motivation*. New York: Van Nostrand, 1928. Pp. xiv+521.
32. Woodworth, R. S. *Dynamic Psychology*. New York: Columbia Univ. Press, 1918. Pp. 210.
33. ———. Dynamic psychology. Chap. 5 in Psychologies of 1925. Worcester, Mass.: Clark Univ. Press, 1926. Pp. 111-126.
34. ———. *Psychology*. (Rev. ed.) New York: Holt, 1929. Pp. 590.

3

The Functional Autonomy of Motives

Gordon W. Allport
Harvard University

For fifty years this JOURNAL has served both as a rich repository for research and as a remarkably sensitive record of the psychological temper of the times. These two services are of great historical value. Since there is no reason to doubt that *The American Journal* will continue to hold its position of leadership in the future, one wonders what new currents of psychological interest its pages will reflect in the coming half-century. With what problems will psychologists be chiefly concerned? What discoveries will they make? What types of scientific formulation will they prefer?

To predict at least one of these trends accurately requires no clairvoyance. On all sides we see the rising tide of interest in problems of personality. Up to a few years ago the somewhat segregated field of clinical psychology alone was concerned; but now theoretical and experimental psychology are likewise deeply affected. As never before the traditional portrait of the "generalized human mind" is being tested against the living models from which it is derived. As compared with particular minds it is found to lack locus, self-consciousness, organic character, and reciprocal interpenetration of parts, all of which are essential to personality. Unless I am greatly mistaken the coming half-century will see many attempts to replace the abstract datum (mind-in-general) with the concrete datum (mind-in-particular), even at the peril of a revolutionary upset in the conception of psychology as *science*.

Some of the best known definitions of psychology

Reprinted from the *American Journal of Psychology*, 1937, with the permission of the publishers and the author.

formulated in the past fifty years have given explicit recognition to the individuality of mind—that is, to its dependence upon the person. But these definitions have not as yet noticeably affected the abstractive tendency of psychological research—not even that of their authors. Wundt, James, and Titchener serve as examples. The first wrote: "It [psychology] *investigates the total content of experience in its relations to the subject.*" The second: "*Psychology is the science of finite individual minds;*" and the third: "*Psychology is the study of experience considered as dependent on some person.*" None of these authors developed his account of mental life to accord with his definition. It is as though some vague sense of propriety guided them in framing their definitions; they *knew* that mind (as a psychological datum) exists only in finite and in personal forms. Yet their historical positions—the spirit of the times in which they worked—prevented them from following their own definitions to the end. Had any one of them done so, the psychology of personality would have had early and illustrious sponsorship.

In line with what I regard as a certain development in the psychology of the future I venture to submit a paper dealing, I think, with the one issue that above all others divides the study of mind-in-general from the study of mind-in-particular. Motivation is the special theme, but the principle involved reaches into every nook and cranny of the evolving science of personality.[1]

TWO KINDS OF DYNAMIC PSYCHOLOGY

Any type of psychology that treats *motives,* thereby endeavoring to answer the question as to *why* men behave as they do, is called a *dynamic psychology.* By its very nature it cannot be merely a descriptive psychology, content to depict the *what* and the *how* of human behavior. The boldness of dynamic psychology in striking for causes stands in marked contrast to the timid, "more scientific," view that seeks nothing else than the estab-

[1] What follows is drawn in part from Chapter VII of my forthcoming book, *Personality: A Psychological Interpretation,* 1937.

lishment of a mathematical function for the relation
between some artificially simple stimulus and some
equally artificial and simple response. If the psychology
of personality is to be more than a matter of coefficients
of correlation it too must be a dynamic psychology, and
seek first and foremost a sound and adequate theory of
the nature of human dispositions.

The type of dynamic psychology almost universally
held, though sufficient from the point of view of the
abstract motives of the generalized mind, fails to provide
a foundation solid enough to bear the weight of any
single full-bodied personality. The reason is that prevailing dynamic doctrines refer every mature motive of
personality to underlying original instincts, wishes, or
needs, shared *by all men*. Thus, the concert artist's devotion to his music is sometimes 'explained' as an extension of his self-assertive instinct, of the need for sentience,
or as a symptom of some repressed striving of the libido.
In McDougall's hormic psychology, for example, it is
explicitly stated that only the instincts or propensities
can be prime movers. Though capable of extension (on
both the receptive and executive sides), they are always
few in number, common in all men, and established at
birth. The enthusiastic collector of bric-a-brac derives his
enthusiasm from the parental instinct; so too does the
kindly old philanthropist, as well as the mother of a
brood. It does not matter how different these three interests may seem to be, they derive their energy from
the same source. The principle is that a very few basic
motives suffice for explaining the endless varieties of
human interests. The psychoanalyst holds the same oversimplified theory. The number of human interests that
he regards as so many canalizations of the one basic
sexual instinct is past computation.

The authors of this type of dynamic psychology are
concerning themselves only with mind-in-general. They
seek a classification of the common and basic motives
by which to explain both normal or neurotic behavior of
any individual case. (This is true even though they may
regard their own list as heuristic or even as fictional.)
The plan really does not work. The very fact that the
lists are so different in their composition suggests—what

to a naïve observer is plain enough—that motives are almost infinitely varied among men, not only in form but in substance. Not four wishes, nor eighteen propensities, nor any and all combinations of these, even with their extensions and variations, seem adequate to account for the endless variety of goals sought by an endless variety of mortals. Paradoxically enough, in many personalities the few simplified needs or instincts alleged to be the *common* ground for all motivation, turn out to be completely lacking.

The second type of dynamic psychology, the one here defended, regards adult motives as infinitely varied, and as self-sustaining, *contemporary* systems, growing out of antecedent systems, but functionally independent of them. Just as a child gradually repudiates his dependence on his parents, develops a will of his own, becomes self-active and self-determining, and outlives his parents, so it is with motives. Each motive has a definite point of origin which may possibly lie in instincts, or, more likely, in the organic tensions of infancy. Chronologically speaking, all adult purposes can be traced back to these seed-forms in infancy, but as the individual matures the tie is broken. Whatever bond remains, is historical, not functional.

Such a theory is obviously opposed to psychoanalysis and to all other genetic accounts that assume inflexibility in the root purposes and drives of life. (Freud says that the structure of the Id *never* changes!) The theory declines to admit that the energies of adult personality are infantile or archaic in nature. Motivation is *always* contemporary. The life of modern Athens is *continuous* with the life of the ancient city, but it in no sense *depends* upon its present "go." The life of a tree is continuous with that of its seed, but the seed no longer sustains and nourishes the full grown tree. Earlier purposes lead into later purposes, and are abandoned in their favor.

William James taught a curious doctrine that has been a matter for incredulous amusement ever since, the doctrine of the *transitoriness of instincts*. According to this theory—not so quaint as sometimes thought—an instinct appears but once in a lifetime, whereupon it promptly disappears through its transformation into habits. If there *are* instincts this is no doubt of their fate, for no instinct can retain its motivational force unimpaired after it has been absorbed and recast under the transforming influence of learning. Such is the reasoning of James, and such is the logic of functional autonomy. The psychology of personality must be a psychology of *post-instinctive* behavior.

Woodworth has spoken of the transformation of "mechanisms" into "drives." [2] A mechanism Woodworth defines as any course of behavior that brings about an adjustment. A *drive* is any neural process that releases mechanisms especially concerned with consummatory reactions. In the course of learning, many preparatory mechanisms must be developed in order to lead to the consummation of an original purpose. These mechanisms are the effective cause of activity in each succeeding mechanism, furnishing the drive for each stage following in the series. Originally all these mechanisms were merely instrumental, only links in the long chain of processes involved in the achievement of an *instinctive* purpose; with time and development, with integration and elaboration, many of these mechanisms become activated directly, setting up a state of desire and tension for activities and objects no longer connected with the original impulse. Activities and objects that earlier in the game were *means* to an end, now become *ends* in themselves.[3]

Although Woodworth's choice of quasi-neurological

[2] R. S. Woodworth, *Dynamic Psychology*, 1918. Equivalent assertions are those of W. Stern concerning the transformation of "phenomotives" into "genomotives" (*Allegemeine Psychologie*, 1935, 569), and of E. C. Tolman regarding the "strangle hold" that "means-objects" acquire by "setting up in their own right" (Psychology versus immediate experience, *Phil. Sci.*, 2, 1935, 370).

[3] "The fundamental drive towards a certain end may be hunger, sex, pugnacity or what not, but once the activity is started, the means to the end becomes an object of interest on its own account" (Woodworth, *op. cit.*, 201). "The primal forces of hunger, fear, sex, and the rest, continue in force, but do not by any means, even with their combinations, account for the sum total of drives activating the experienced individual" (*ibid.*, 104).

terminology is not the best, his doctrine, or one like it is indispensable in accounting for the infinite number of effective motives possible in human life, and for their severance from the rudimentary desires of infancy. Further discussion of the operation of the principle and a critique of Woodworth's position will be more to the point after a review of the evidence in favor of the principle.

EVIDENCE FOR FUNCTIONAL AUTONOMY

We begin in a common sense way. An ex-sailor has a craving for the sea, a musician longs to return to his instrument after an enforced absence, a city-dweller yearns for his native hills, and a miser continues to amass his useless horde. Now, the sailor may have first acquired his love for the sea as an incident in his struggle to earn a living. The sea was merely a conditioned stimulus associated with satisfaction of his 'nutritional craving.' But now the ex-sailor is perhaps a wealthy banker; the original motive is destroyed; and yet the hunger for the sea persists unabated, even increases in intensity as it becomes more remote from the 'nutritional segment.' The musician may first have been stung by a rebuke or by a slur on his inferior performances into mastering his instrument, but now he is safely beyond the power of these taunts; there is no need to compensate further; now he loves his instrument more than anything else in the world. Once indeed the city dweller may have associated the hills around his mountain home with nutritional and erotogenic satisfactions, but these satisfactions he now finds in his city home, *not* in the mountains; whence then comes all his hill-hunger? The miser perhaps learned his habits of thrift in dire necessity, or perhaps his thrift was a symptom of sexual perversion (as Freud would claim), and yet the miserliness persists, and even becomes stronger with the years, even after the necessity or the roots of the neurosis have been relieved.

Workmanship is a good example of functional autonomy. A good workman feels compelled to do clean-cut jobs even though his security, or the praise of others, no longer depends upon high standards. In fact, in a day of jerry-building his workman-like standards may be to his economic disadvantage. Even so he cannot do a slipshod job. Workmanship is not an instinct, but so firm is the hold it may acquire on a man that it is little wonder Veblen mistook it for one. A business man, long since secure economically, works himself into ill-health, and sometimes even back into poverty, for the sake of carrying on his plans. What was once an instrumental technique becomes a master-motive.

Neither necessity nor reason can make one contented permanently on a lonely island or on an isolated farm after one is adapted to active, energetic city life. The acquired habits seem sufficient to urge one to a frenzied existence, even though reason and health demand the simpler life.

The pursuit of literature, the development of good taste in clothes, the use of cosmetics, the acquiring of an automobile, strolls in the public park, or a winter in Miami—all may first serve, let us say, the interests of sex. But every one of these instrumental activities may become an interest in itself, held for a life time, long after the erotic motive has been laid away in lavender. People often find that they have lost allegiance to their original aims because of their deliberate preference for the many ways of achieving them.

The maternal sentiment offers a final illustration. Many young mothers bear their children unwillingly, dismayed at the thought of the drudgery of the future. At first they may be indifferent to, or even hate, their offspring; the 'parental instinct' seems wholly lacking. The only motives that hold such a mother to child-tending may be fear of what her critical neighbors will say, fear of the law, a habit of doing any job well, or perhaps a dim hope that the child will provide security for her in her old age. However gross these motives, they are sufficient to hold her to her work, until through the practice of devotion her burden becomes a joy. As her love for the child develops, her earlier practical motives are forgotten. In later years not one of these original motives may operate. The child may be incompetent, criminal, a disgrace to her, and far from serving as a staff for her declining years, he may continue to drain her resources and vitality. The neighbors may criticize her for indulging the child, the law may exonerate her from allegiance; she certainly feels no pride in such a child; yet she sticks to him. The tenacity of the maternal sentiment under such adversity is proverbial.

Such examples from everyday experience could be multiplied *ad infinitum*. The evidence, however, appears in sharper outline when it is taken from experimental and clinical studies. In each of the following instances some new function emerges as an independently structured unit from preceding functions. The activity of these new units does not depend upon the continued activity of the units from which they developed.

(1) *The circular reflex.* Everyone has observed the almost endless repetition of acts by a child. The goodnatured parent who picks up a spoon repeatedly thrown down by a baby wearies of this occupation long before the infant does. Such repetitive behavior, found likewise in early vocalization (babbling), and in other early forms of play, is commonly ascribed to the mechanism of the circular reflex.[4] It is an elementary instance of functional autonomy; for any situation where the consummation of an act provides adequate stimulation for the repetition of the *same* act does not require any backward tracing of motives. The act is self-perpetuating until it is inhibited by new activities or fatigue.

(2) *Conative perseveration.* Many experiments show that incompleted tasks set up tensions that tend to keep the individual at work until they are resolved. No hypothesis of self-assertion, rivalry, or any other basic need, is required. The completion of the task itself has become a quasi-need with dynamic force of its own. It has been shown, for example, that interrupted tasks are better remembered than completed tasks,[5] that an individual interrupted in a task will, even in the face of considerable opposition return to that task,[6] that even trivial tasks

[4] E. B. Holt, *Animal Drive and the Learning Process*, 1931, esp. Chaps. VII and VIII.

[5] B. Zeigarnik, Über das Behalten von erledigten und unerledigten Handlungen, *Psychol. Forsch.*, 9, 1927, 1-86.

[6] M. Ovsiankina, Die Wiederaufnahme unterbrochener Handlungen, *ibid.*, 11, 1928, 302-379.

undertaken in a casual way become almost haunting in character until they are completed.[7]

Conative perseveration of this order is stronger if an empty interval of time follows the period of work, showing that *left to itself*, without the inhibiting effect of other duties or activities, the motive grows stronger and stronger. The experiment of Kendig proves this point, as well as that of C. E. Smith.[8] The latter investigator demonstrated that there is more success in removing a conditioned fear if the de-conditioning process is commenced immediately. After a twenty-four hour delay the fear has become set, and is more difficult to eradicate. Hence the sound advice to drivers of automobiles or airplanes who have been involved in an accident, that they drive again immediately to conquer the shock of the accident, lest the fear become set into a permanent phobia. The rule seems to be that unless specifically inhibited all emotional shocks, given time to set, tend to take on a compulsive autonomous character.

(3) *Conditioned reflexes not requiring reënforcement.* The pure conditioned reflex readily dies out unless the secondary stimulus is occasionally reënforced by the primary stimulus. The dog does not continue to salivate whenever it hears a bell unless sometimes at least an edible offering accompanies the bell. But there are innumerable instances in human life where a single association, *never* reënforced, results in the establishment of a life-long dynamic system. An experience associated only once with a bereavement, an accident, or a battle, may become the center of a permanent phobia or complex, not in the least dependent on a recurrence of the original shock.

(4) *Counterparts in animal behavior.* Though the validity of a principle in human psychology never depends upon its having a counterpart in animal psychology, still it is of interest to find functional autonomy in the lower organisms. For example, rats, who will first

[7] I. Kendig, Studies in perseveration, *J. Psychol.*, 3, 1936, 223-264.

[8] C. E. Smith, Change in the apparent resistance of the skin as a function of certain physiological and psychological factors, A thesis deposited in the Harvard College Library, 1934.

learn a certain habit only under the incentive of some specific tension, as hunger, will, after learning, often perform the habit even when fed to repletion.[9]

Another experiment shows that rats trained to follow a long and difficult path, will for a time persist in using this path, even though a short easy path to the goal is offered and even after the easier path has been learned.[10] Among rats as among human beings, old and useless habits have considerable power in their own right.

Olson studied the persistence of artificially induced scratching habits in rats. Collodion applied to the ears of the animal set up removing and cleaning movements. Four days later the application was repeated. From that time on the animals showed significantly greater number of cleaning movements than control animals. A month after the beginning of the experiment when the ears of the rats as studied by the microscope showed no further trace of irritation, the number of movements was still very great. Whether the induced habit spasm was permanently retained the experimenter does not say.[11]

(5) *Rhythm.* A rat whose activity bears a definite relation to his habits of feeding (being greatest just preceding a period of feeding and midway between two such periods) will, even when starved, display the same periodicity and activity. The acquired rhythm persists without dependence on the original periodic stimulation of feeding.[12]

Even a mollusc whose habits of burrowing in the sand and reappearing depend upon the movements of the tide, will, when removed from the beach to the laboratory, continue for several days in the same rhythm with-

[9] J. D. Dodgson, Relative values of reward and punishment in habit formation, *Psychobiol.*, 1, 1917, 231-276. This work has already been interpreted by K. S. Lashley as favoring Woodworth's dynamic theory as opposed to Freud's (Contributions of Freudism to psychology: III. Physiological analysis of the libido, *Psychol. Rev.*, 31, 1924, 192-202).

[10] H. C. Gilhousen, Fixation of excess distance patterns in the white rat, *J. Comp. Psychol.*, 16, 1933, 1-23.

[11] W. C. Olson, *The Measurement of Nervous Habits in Normal Children*, 1929, 62-65.

[12] C. P. Richter, A behavioristic study of the activity of the rat, *Comp. Psychol. Monog.*, 1, 1922, (no. 2), 1-55.

out the tide. Likewise certain animals, with nocturnal rhythms advantageous in avoiding enemies, obtaining food, or preventing excessive evaporation from the body, may exhibit such rhythms even when kept in a laboratory with constant conditions of illumination, humidity, and temperature.[13]

There are likewise instances where acquired rhythms in human life have taken on a dynamic character. Compulsive neurotics enter upon fugues or debauches, apparently not because of specific stimulation, but because "the time has come." A dipsomaniac, in confinement and deprived for months of his alcohol, describes the fierceness of the recurrent appetite (obviously acquired) as follows.

> Those craving paroxysms occur at regular intervals, three weeks apart, lasting for several days. They are not weak, nambypamby things for scoffers to laugh at. If not assuaged with liquor they become spells of physical and mental illness. My mouth drools saliva, my stomach and intestines seem cramped, and I become bilious, nauseated, and in a shaky nervous funk.[14]

In such states of drug addition, as likewise in states of hunger, lust, fatigue, there is to be sure a physical craving, but the rhythms of the craving are partially acquired, and are always accentuated by the mental habits associated with it. For instance, eating in our civilized way of life takes place not because physical hunger naturally occurs three times a day, but because of habitual rhythms of expectancy. The habit of smoking is much more than a matter of craving for the specific narcotic effects of tobacco; it is a craving for the motor ritual and periodic distraction as well.

(6) *Neuroses.* Why are acquired tics, stammering, sexual perversions, phobias, and anxiety so stubborn and so often incurable? Even psychoanalysis, with its deepest of depth-probing, seldom succeeds in effecting *complete*

---

[13] S. C. Crawford, The habits and characteristics of nocturnal animals, *Quart. Rev. Biol.*, 9, 1934, 201-214.

[14] Inmate Ward Eight, *Beyond the Door of Delusion*, 1932, 281.

cures in such cases, even though the patient may feel relieved or at least reconciled to his difficulties after treatment. The reason seems to be that what are usually called 'symptoms' are in reality something more. They have set themselves up in their own right as independent systems of motivation. Merely disclosing their roots does not change their independent activity.[15]

(7) *The relation between ability and interest.* Psychometric studies have shown that the relation between ability and interest is always positive, often markedly so. A person likes to do what he can do well. Over and over again it has been demonstrated that the skill learned for some external reason, turns into an interest, and is self-propelling, even though the original reason for pursuing it has been lost. A student who at first undertakes a field of study in college because it is prescribed, because it pleases his parents, or because it comes at a convenient hour, often ends by finding himself absorbed, perhaps for life, in the subject itself. He is not happy without it. The original motives are entirely lost. What was a means to an end has become an end in itself.

Furthermore, there is the case of genius. A skill takes possession of the man. No primitive motivation is needed to account for his persistent, absorbed activity. It just *is* the alpha and omega of life to him. It is impossible to think of Pasteur's concern for health, food, sleep, or family, as the root of his devotion to his work. For long periods of time he was oblivious of them all, losing himself in the white heat of research for which he had been trained and in which he had *acquired* a compelling and absorbing interest.

A much more modest instance is the finding of indus-

---

[15] The case of W. E. Leonard, *The Locomotive God*, 1927, is instructive in this regard. An intense phobia was not relieved by tracing its history backward to the start of life. Even though he could explain why he was once frightened for a very good reason (by a locomotive), the author is quite unable to explain why now he is frightened *for no particular reason*. Such neuroses, and psychotic delusional systems as well, often acquire a "strangle hold," and the task of dislodging them is usually more than therapeutic skill is equal to.

trial research that when special incentives are offered and work speeded up as a consequence, and then these special incentives removed, *the work continues at the speeded rate*. The habit of working at a faster tempo persists without external support.

(8) *Sentiments vs. instincts*. Every time an alleged instinct can by rigid analysis be demonstrated not to be innate but acquired, there is in this demonstration evidence for functional autonomy. It is true enough that maternal conduct, gregariousness, curiosity, workmanship, and the like, have the tenacity and compelling power that instincts are supposed to have. If they are not instincts, then they must be autonomous sentiments with as much dynamic character as has been attributed to instincts. It is not necessary here to review all the arguments in favor of regarding such alleged instincts as acquired sentiments.

(9) *The dynamic character of personal values*. When an interest-system has once been formed it not only creates a tensional condition that may be readily aroused, leading to overt conduct in some way satisfying to the interest, but it also acts as a silent agent for selecting and directing any behavior related to it. Take the case of people with strongly marked esthetic interests. Experiments with the word-association test have shown that such people respond more quickly to stimulus-words connected with this interest than to words relating to interests they lack.[16] Likewise, in scanning a newspaper they will observe and remember more items pertaining to art; they also take a greater interest in clothes than do non-esthetic people; and when they are asked to rate the virtues of others, they place esthetic qualities high. In short the existence of a well-established acquired interest exerts a directive and determining effect on conduct just as is to be expected of any dynamic system. The evidence can be duplicated for many interests other than the esthetic.[17]

[16] H. Cantril, General and specific attitudes, *Psychol. Monog.*, 42, 1932, (no. 192), 1-109.

[17] H. Cantril and G. W. Allport, Recent applications of the *study of values, J. Abnorm. & Soc. Psychol.*, 28, 1933, 259-273.

CRITIQUE OF FUNCTIONAL AUTONOMY

Objections to the principle of autonomy may be expected from two sides. Behaviorists will continue to prefer their conception of organic drive with its capacity for manifold conditioning by ever receding stimuli. Whereas purposivists will be unwilling to accept a pluralistic principle that seems to leave motives so largely at the mercy of learning.

The behaviorist is well satisfied with motivation in terms of organic drive and conditioning because he feels that he somehow has secure anchorage in physiological structure. (The closer he approaches physiological structure the happier the behaviorist is.) But the truth of the matter is that the neural physiology of organic drive and conditioning is no better established, and no easier to imagine, than is the neural physiology of the type of complex autonomous units of motivation here described.

Two behavioristic principles will be said to account adequately for the instances of functional autonomy previously cited, viz., the circular reflex and cross-conditioning. The former concept, acceptable enough when applied to infant behavior, merely says that the more activity a muscle engages in, the more activity of the same sort does it engender through a self-sustaining circuit.[18] This is, to be sure, a clear instance of autonomy, albeit on a primitive level, oversimplified so far as adult conduct is concerned. The doctrine of cross-conditioning refers to subtle recession of stimuli, and to the intricate possibility of cross-connections in conditioning. For instance, such ubiquitous external stimuli as humidity, daylight, gravitation, may feed collaterally into open channels of activity, arousing mysteriously and unexpectedly a form of conduct to which they have unconsciously been conditioned. For example, the angler whose fishing expeditions have been accompanied by sun, wind, or a balmy June day, may feel a desire to go fishing whenever the barometer, the thermometer, or the calendar in his city home tells him that these conditions prevail.[19]

[18] E. B. Holt, op. cit., 38.
[19] Ibid., 224.

Innumerable such crossed stimuli are said to account for the arousal of earlier patterns of activity.

Such a theory inherits, first of all, the well-known difficulties resident in the principle of conditioning whenever it is made the sole explanation of human behavior. Further, though the reflex circle and cross-conditioning may in fact exist, they are really rather trivial principles. They leave the formation of interest and its occasional arousal almost entirely to chance factors of stimulation. They give no picture at all of the spontaneous and variable aspects of traits, interests, or sentiments. These dispositions are regarded as purely *reactive* in nature; the stimulus is all-important. The truth is that dispositions *sort out* stimuli congenial to them, and this activity does not in the least resemble the rigidity of reflex response.[20]

A variant on the doctrine of cross-conditioning is the principle of redintegration.[21] This concept admits the existence of highly integrated dispositions of a neuropsychic order. These dispositions can be aroused *as a whole* by any stimulus previously associated with their functioning. In this theory likewise, the disposition is regarded as a rather passive affair, waiting for reactivation by some portion of the original stimulus. Here again the variability of the disposition and its urge-like quality are not accounted for. The stimulus is thought merely to reinstate a complex determining tendency. Nothing is said about how the stimuli themselves are *selected*, why a motive once aroused becomes insistent, surmounting obstacles, skillfully subordinating conflicting impulses, and inhibiting irrelevant trains of thought.

In certain respects the principle of autonomy stands midway between the behavioristic view and the thoroughgoing purposive psychology of the hormic order. It agrees

[20] The basic fact that complex "higher" centers have the power of inhibiting, selecting, and initiating the activity of simpler segmental responses is a fact too well established to need elaboration here. It constitutes the very foundation of the psychophysiological theories advanced by Sherrington, Herrick, Dodge, Köhler, Troland, and many others.

[21] Cf. H. L. Hollingworth, *Psychology of the Functional Neuroses*, 1920.

with the former in emphasizing the acquisition of motives, in avoiding an a priori and unchanging set of original urges, and in recognizing (as limited principles) the operation of the circular response and cross-conditioning. It agrees with the hormic psychologist, however, in finding that striving-from-within is a far more essential characteristic of motive than stimulation-from-without. It agrees likewise in distrusting the emphasis upon stomach contractions and other "excess and deficit stimuli" as "causes" of mature behavior. Such segmental sources of energy even when conditioned cannot possibly account for the "go" of conduct. But functional autonomy does not rely as does hormic theory upon modified instinct, which after all is as archaic a principle as the conditioning of autonomic segmental tensions, but upon the capacity of human beings to replenish their energy through a plurality of constantly changing systems of a dynamic order.

The hormic psychologist, however, will not accept the autonomy of new motivational systems. If mechanisms can turn into drives, he asks, why is it that habits and skills as they become exercised to the point of perfection do not acquire an ever increasing driving force? [22] The mechanisms of walking, speaking, or dressing, cannot be said to furnish their own motive-power. One walks, speaks, or dresses in order to satisfy a motive entirely external to these learned skills.[23]

The criticism is sufficiently cogent to call into question Woodworth's form of stating the principle, viz., "mechanisms may become drives." It is not an adequate statement of the case.

Looking at the issue more closely it seems to be neither the perfected talent nor the automatic habit that has driving power, but the imperfect talent and the habit-in-the-making. The child who is *just learning* to speak,

[22] W. McDougall, Motives in the light of recent discussion, *Mind*, 29, 1920, 277-293.

[23] Though this objection is usually valid, it is not always so, for there are cases where the liking for walks, for talking for the sake of talking, or for dressing, playing games, etc., seems to be a self-sustaining motivational system.

to walk, or to dress is, in fact, likely to engage in these activities for their own sake, precisely as does the adult who has an *unfinished* task in hand. He remembers it, returns to it, and suffers a feeling of frustration if he is prevented from engaging in it. Motives are always a kind of striving for some form of completion; they are unresolved tension, and demand a "closure" to activity under way. (Latent motives are dispositions that are easily thrown by a stimulus or by a train of associations into this state of active tension.) The active motive subsides when its goal is reached, or in the case of a motor skill, when it has become at last automatic. The novice in automobile driving has an unquestionable impulse to master the skill. Once acquired the ability sinks to the level of an *instrumental* disposition and is aroused only in the service of some other *driving* (unfulfilled) motive.

Now, in the case of the permanent interests of personality, the situation is the same. A man whose motive is to acquire learning, or to perfect his craft, can never be satisfied that he has reached the end of his quest, for his problems are never completely solved, his skill is never perfect. Lasting interests are recurrent sources of discontent, and from their incompleteness they derive their forward impetus. Art, science, religion, love, are never perfected. Motor skills, however, are often perfected, and beyond that stage they seldom provide their own motive power. It is, then, only mechanisms-on-the-make (in process of perfecting) that serve as drives. With this emendation, Woodworth's view is corrected, and McDougall's objection is met.[24]

IMPLICATIONS OF FUNCTIONAL AUTONOMY

The principle of functional autonomy accounts, as no other principle of dynamic psychology is able to do, for the concrete impulses that lie at the root of personal

---

[24] This theory embraces very easily the work of K. Lewin and his associates upon the nature of "quasi-needs." The urgency of these needs is greatest just before a goal is reached, after which time the motive subsides completely.

behavior. It is thus the first step in establishing a basis for the more realistic study of unique and individual forms for personality. "But how—" the traditionalists may cry, "how are we ever to have a *science* of unique events? Science must generalize." So it must, but it is a manifest error to assume that a general principle of motivation must involve the postulation of abstract or general motives. What the objectors forget is that *a general law may be a law that tells how uniqueness comes about*. The principle of functional autonomy is general enough to meet the needs of science, but particularized enough in its operation to account for the uniqueness of personal conduct. Its specific advantages stand out in the following summary.

(1) It clears the way for a completely dynamic psychology of *traits, attitudes, interests,* and *sentiments,* which can now be regarded as the ultimate and true dispositions of the mature personality.

(2) It avoids the absurdity of regarding the energy of life now, in the *present,* as somehow consisting of early archaic forms (instincts, prepotent reflexes, or the never-changing Id). Learning brings new systems of interests into existence just as it does new abilities and skills. At each stage of development these interests are always contemporary; whatever drives, drives *now.*

(3) It dethrones the stimulus. A motive is no longer regarded as a mechanical reflex or as a matter of redintegration, depending entirely upon the capricious operation of a conditioned stimulus. In a very real sense dispositions *select* the stimuli to which they respond, even though *some* stimulus is required for their arousal.

(4) It readily admits the validity of all other established principles of growth. Functional autonomy recognizes the products of differentiation, integration, maturation, exercise, imitation, suggestion, conditioning, trauma, and all other processes of development; and allows, as they do not, considered by themselves, for the preservation of these products in significant motivational patterns.

(5) It places in proper perspective the problems of the origin of conduct by removing the fetish of the

genetic method. Not that the historical view of behavior is unimportant for a complete understanding of personality, but so far as *motives* are concerned the cross-sectional dynamic analysis is more significant. Motives being always contemporary should be studied in their present structure. Failure to do so is probably the chief reason why psychoanalysis meets so many defeats, as do all other therapeutic schemes relying too exclusively upon uncovering the motives of early childhood.

(6) It accounts for the force of delusions, shell-shock, phobias, and all manner of compulsive and maladaptive behavior. One would expect such unrealistic modes of adjustment to be given up as they are shown to be poor ways of confronting the environment. Insight and the law of effect should both remove them—but too often they have acquired a strangle hold in their own right.

(7) At last we can account adequately for socialized and civilized behavior. The principle supplies the correction necessary to the faulty logic of *bellum omnium contra omnes*. Starting life, as a completely selfish being, the child would indeed remain entirely wolfish and piggish throughout his days unless genuine transformations of motives took place. Motives being completely alterable, the dogma of Egoism turns out to be a callow and superficial philosophy of behavior, or else a useless redundancy.

(8) It explains likewise why a person often *becomes* what at first he merely *pretends* to be—the smiling professional hostess who grows fond of her once irksome rôle and is unhappy when deprived of it; the man who for so long has counterfeited the appearance of self-confidence and optimism that he is always driven to assume it; the prisoner who comes to love his shackles. Such *personae*, as Jung observes, are often transformed into the real self. The mask becomes the *anima*.

(9) The drive behind genius is explained. Gifted people demand the exercise of their talents, even when no other reward lies ahead. In lesser degree the various hobbies, the artistic, or the intellectual interests of any person show the same significant autonomy.

(10) In brief, the principle of functional autonomy is a declaration of independence for the psychology of per-

sonality. Though in itself a general law, at the same time it helps to account, not for the abstract motivation of an impersonal and therefore non-existent mind-in-general, but for the concrete, viable motives of each and every mind-in-particular.

4

Facts Which Support the Concept of Need or Drive

HENRY A. MURRAY

Harvard University

A concept of motivational processes within the organism is necessarily hypothetical, since no such processes can be directly perceived by the senses. If they do occur, only their manifestations will be observable. Furthermore, since every actual occasion is the outcome of many concatenating variables, in order to be relatively certain of the presence and strength of any single factor one must be able to distinguish and approximately measure most of the others, both within and without the organism. Though such a comprehensive formulation of an event may never be achieved in psychology, this is the goal, I believe, towards which experimentalists should bend their efforts.

Psychologists are divided on the question of whether it is possible to formulate behaviour without a "motivational force" variable. This controversy, which may be termed the reflex *vs.* drive controversy, is just another variety of the age-old opposition between two schools of thought, morphic factualism and ergic conceptualism. Perhaps most scientists agree that both principles must be represented in any adequate schematization of events, but in the discussion of any concrete problem differences in emphasis inevitably arise: structure *vs.* force, form *vs.* function, mechanism *vs.* dynamism. The supposition is hardly to be avoided that these radical differences in intellectual bias are based upon underlying differences in personality. Since this is the testimony of experience, I

Reprinted from the *Journal of Psychology*, Vol. 3, 1937, with permission of the author and the publishers.

should be a poor psychologist, indeed, if I did not suspect that I myself had been prompted to observe and assemble the facts which seem to necessitate a dynamic concept by some temperamental, or sentimental, prejudice. Likewise, I should be living in an unreal world if I thought that any facts and arguments of mine could modify a well entrenched contrasting theory. An established scheme is the support and comfort of an intellectual man and he is as anxious for its permanency as a sea captain is for the welfare of his barque. Experience teaches us that the usual result of a battle of words is a firmer allegiance of each opponent to the theory that he originally advocated.

My own opinion is that an adequate theory must give *both* mechanism and dynamism their proper place in the scheme of things, but in this paper I am limiting myself to facts which, it seems to me, cannot be formulated or brought into relation with other facts without a dynamic principle. I have no hope of convicing the opposition, but I may give support to the dynamicists, and, by appealing to the phenomena, convince minds which are fresh and supple enough to bend without breaking.

Two commonly used terms for a motivational process are *drive* and *need*, and, since I cannot see that one is to be preferred to the other, I shall regard them as synonymous and use them interchangeably.

Need is a concept to account for certain objective and subjective facts. Roughly speaking, objective facts are occurrences in the external world which may be publicly perceived through the senses—the manifest bodily movements and words of a subject. Subjective facts, on the other hand, are inner experiences—visceral sensations, emotions, images, desires and thought processes—of which only the subject is aware, but which may be communicated to an investigator as they occur or in retrospect. If the facts which the concept of need has been constructed to explain, are other than what we have observed, then the concept must be re-defined or abolished.

If we start with objective behavioural facts we shall be aligning ourselves with scientists in other fields, and, what is more, shall be on firmer ground, for it is easier to agree about objective facts than about subjective facts.

In starting with a consideration of behaviour we suppose that we are focussing upon one of the most significant aspects of the organism, and hence of the personality. For upon behaviour and its results depends everything which is generally regarded as important—physical well-being and survival, development and achievement, happiness and the perpetuation of the species. Of course, we are not interested in overt behaviour to the exclusion of other aspects—inner conflicts, feelings, emotions, sentiments, fantasies and beliefs. But, in accord with many psychologists, we believe that it is best to start with behaviour. And, since it is my aim to describe behaviour rather than the external factors which determine it, I shall, for the present, have little to say about the nature of the environment.

We must, of course, start by limiting ourselves to a definite temporal unit—a temporal unit which holds together psychologically and is marked off by a more or less clear cut beginning and ending. For such a behavioural event it seems that the simplest formula that can be devised—and let us hope that it is not a gross oversimplification—is as follows:

$$B.S. \rightarrow A \rightarrow E.S.$$

where $B.S.$ stands for the conditions that exist at the initiation of activity; $E.S.$ for the conditions that exist at the cessation of activity; and A for the action patterns—motor or verbal—of the organism. The difference between $B.S.$ and $E.S.$ (what might be called the B-E form of the behaviour event) describes the *effect* which has been produced by the action patterns.

ACTONES AND EFFECTS

No matter how a behavioural event is analyzed, whether it is taken as a whole (molar description), or whether it is analyzed into parts (molecular description), the action patterns (mechanisms of the organism) and the B-E form (effect produced) can be distinguished. One may always ask, "What is done?" (*i.e.,* "What effect is produced?") or, "How is it done?" (*i.e.,* "What means were used?"). These two objectively apparent aspects of a behavioural event, though always intimately connected, may and should be clearly distinguished. For instance:

B.S. $\rightarrow$	A $\rightarrow$	E.S.
(1) Food placed before a child with an empty stomach	Crying, followed by swallowing of food that is offered by mother	Food in the stomach.
(2) Food placed before a child with an empty stomach	Eating with a knife and fork	Food in the stomach.

The *B-E* forms in the two events are similar, but the action patterns are entirely different.

Though the introduction of new terms is sometimes very annoying to others and should be avoided if possible, I need, at this point, a single term which will refer only to bodily movements as such (the mechanisms, means, ways, modes) and not at all to the effects of such movements. The word "action" cannot be used because it is commonly employed to describe both the movements and the effects of the movements. Hoping, then, for the reader's tolerance, I shall introduce the term *actone* to stand for any action pattern *qua* action pattern. And, since action patterns are mostly of two sorts, I shall divide *actones* into: motones (muscular-motor action patterns) and verbones (verbal action patterns).

A motone is a temporal series of more or less organized muscular contractions and a verbone is a temporal series of more or less organized words or written symbols. The verbone is constituted by the actual words used. The intended, or realized, effect of a verbone is something quite different.

Now, since the first systematic step in the construction of any science is that of classification, we, as students of behaviour, must find proper criteria for distinguishing one form of conduct from another. The problem arises: Shall we classify in terms of actones or in terms of effects? We may, of course, and shall eventually, classify according to both criteria, but the question is, which method is the most profitable for scientific purposes? We can predict that the two classifications will not correspond. According to one method we shall find in each category a number of similar actones, and according to the other method we shall find in each category a number of similar effects. Since it is obvious that similar actones—putting food in the mouth and putting poison in the mouth—may have different effects, and different actones—putting poison in the mouth and pulling the trigger of a revolver—may have similar effects, we shall be describing different aspects of conduct if we classify in the terms of actones than if we classify in terms of effects.

Practical experience has led me to believe that of the two the classification in terms of effects organizes for our understanding something that is more fundamental than what is organized by the classification in terms of actones. Without minimizing the great significance of the latter, I should like briefly to enumerate the reasons for this opinion.

1. Physical survival depends upon the attainment of certain effects; not upon what actones are employed.

If oxygen, water and nutriment are not assimilated or if injurious substances are not avoided, the organism will die.

2. Certain effects are universally attained by living organisms, but the actones that attain them vary greatly from one species to another.

Some organisms kill their prey with teeth and claws, others by injecting venom.

3. During the life history of a single individual certain effects are regularly attained, but the actones change.

The embryo assimilates food through the umbilical vessels, the infant sucks it from the tendered breast of the mother, the child eats with a spoon that is put before him, and the adult has to work, or steal, to get money to buy food.

4. According to the Law of Effect, which is widely accepted in one or another of its modifications, the actones which become habitual are for the most part those which, in the past, have led most directly to the end situations. Hence, effects determine what actones become established.

5. When confronted by a novel situation, an organism commonly persists in its "efforts" to bring about a certain result, but with each frustration it is apt to change its mode of attack. Here, the trend is the constant feature and the mechanism the inconstant.

6. There are some effects which can only be attained by entirely novel actones.

As a rule, laughter is only evoked by a *new* joke.

7. That actones are of secondary importance is shown by the fact that many biologically necessary effects may be brought about by the activity of another person.

This occurs when a nurse ministers to the wants of a sick child.

We may see, I think, from this brief list of observations that certain effects are more fundamental to life and occur more regularly than any observable action patterns. This agrees with Skinner's conclusions. For the latter found in his experiments with rats that if one takes a particular effect—the depression of a lever—as the criterion for the rate of responding, one gets quantitatively lawful results; whereas if one takes a particular actone—for instance, the movement of the rat's right paw (on the lever) one gets irregular and inconsistent figures. In other words, the rat may use one of a number of different movements to depress the lever. The movements, Skinner concludes, are "all equally elicitable by the stimulation arising from the lever, they are *quantitatively mutually replaceable*. The uniformity of the change in rate excludes any supposition that we are dealing with a group of separate reflexes, and forces the conclusion that 'pressing the lever' behaves experimentally as a unitary thing" (6).

In passing, it may be said that the "depression of a lever" is what we should call a subsidiary effect (sub-effect), since, according to the conditions of the experiment, it is an effect which must occur before the major effect—"getting food into the stomach"—is accomplished.

At this point a new concept should be introduced, for there are many acts which, because of some accident or because of the organism's lack of innate or acquired ability, never reach an end situation—that is the total effect (B-E form) is never realized. In such cases, the direction of the movements is usually evident enough, or their preliminary, accessory effects sufficient, to allow an experienced observer to predict with a reasonable degree of accuracy what total effect is being promoted. Such a succession of minor, subsidiary effects (sub-effects) may be called a *trend*. Thus a *trend* describes the direction of movement *away from* the B.S.—movements which, if unembarrassed, would reach a certain kind of E.S. By the use of this concept we may include for classification actions which, though uncompleted, manifest a tendency to achieve a certain end.

THE CONCEPT OF NEED

Now, let us assume that the actual business of classifying in terms of B-E forms has been accomplished. In this classification, each category (B-E form) is merely a phenomenal concept, since it is no more than a general description of a trend exhibited by organisms. In other words, it is merely a collective term for a certain class of occurrences. If we were radical positivists, or if we were primarily concerned with environmental changes, we might stop here. But we are not, and so we ask ourselves: what process or force within the organism brings about the observed effects? We say force because, according to physical theory, all manifest effects of any kind are due to energy overcoming resistance, *i.e.*, force. For the physicist force has now become a measurement of motion—a mere symbol in an equation, but for generations the notion of force as a propelling activity was indispensable to the physicist and, in my opinion, it will be indispensable (*i.e.*, a convenient fiction) to the psychologist for a long time to come. Psychology, in its development, must like the child, pass through certain progressing, though admittedly imperfect, stages and it would be well for the psychologist who believes that he has achieved the sanctity of operationalism to remember that a child does not add a whit to his stature by putting on long pants.

Here we have to do with nervous energy or force, of which we know little, and, therefore, when we use this term in psychology we are referring to something which is analogous to, but not the same as, physical force. We need such a term for it is impossible to construct a dynamical theory without it. We are able to measure differences in the intensity and duration of directed activity. To what may such differences be referred if not to differences in the force of an organic drive? Furthermore, as Lewin has pointed out, the notions of organization and equilibrium necessitates a concept of force. It is always a matter of balance, economy or least action of energy. A number of other considerations favorable to this hypothesis will be advanced later. Are there any adequate reasons for hesitating to do what physical scientists have consistently done before us—conceptualize processes "behind" appearances?

Now, to explain the observed phenomena—the realization of a certain effect—what attributes must be possessed by an organic force? Let us see. It must be something: (a) that is engendered by a certain kind of B.S.; (b) that tends to induce activity—activity which, at first, may be restless and random, but, later, becomes effectively organized; and (c) that tends to persist until a situation (E.S.) is reached which contrasts with the B.S. in certain specific respects. The E.S. *stills* the force which the B.S. *incites*. Thus, the force tends, by inducing a certain trend, to bring about its own resolution.

On the basis of this characterization we may construct a hypothetical entity which we term a *need* (or *drive*). Each need has (a) a typical directional or qualitative, aspect (B-E) form which differentiates it from other needs, as well as (b) an energetic or quantitative aspect, which may be estimated in a variety of ways. Thus, the first and best criterion for distinguishing a certain need is the production by the subject of a certain effect, or, if not this, the occurrence of a certain trend.

Between what we can directly observe—the stimulus and the resulting action—a need is an invisible link, which may be imagined to have the properties that an understanding of the observed phenomena demand. "Need" is, therefore, a *hypothetical* concept.

Strictly speaking, a need is the immediate outcome of certain internal and external occurrences. It comes into being and perishes. It is not a static entity. It is resultant of forces. One need succeeds another. Though each is unique, experience teaches that there are similarities among them, and on the basis of this, needs may be grouped together into classes—each class being, as it were, a single major need. Thus, we may speak of similar needs as being different exhibitions of *one need*, just as when we recognize a friend we do not hesitate to call him by name though he is different from the person with whom we conversed yesterday. Between the different appearances of a certain kind of need there may be nothing to suggest it, but experience and experiment show that if the proper conditions are provided the need (*i.e.*, another manifestation of the same kind of need) will be activated. Thus, we may loosely use the term "need" to refer to an organic potentiality or readiness to respond in a certain way when certain conditions occur. In this sense a need is a latent attribute of an organism. More strictly, it is a noun which stands for the fact that a certain trend is apt to recur.

With successive activations each need tends to become more fixedly associated with the actones which have successfully led to end situations; or, in other words, habits of response commonly become established (mechanization of behaviour). When this occurs "fixation by conditioning" may to some extent replace "need" as an explanatory concept.

The seven arguments which were used to demonstrate the importance of trends and effects are equally favorable to the concept of need, since a need is, by definition, the force within the organism which determines a certain trend or major effect. And now sixteen more arguments in favor of needs may be set down.

8. Complex action is characterized by the occurrence of muscular contractions in widely separate parts of the organism—contractions which manifest synchronous and consecutive coordination. Such organizations of movement must be partially determined by a directional process—which is just what a need, by definition, is. Furthermore, the directional process must occur in some cen-

tral area of communication, because coordination is impossible without communication—in this instance, nervous communication. Thus, the need process must be placed in the brain, for this is the only area to and from which all nerves lead. It is even conceivable that some day there may be instruments for measuring need tension directly.

9. The concept of a directional force within the organism is something to which one may refer differences in the intensity and duration of goal-directed behaviour. The strength of the action cannot be ascribed to the actones *per se*, since these may, and commonly do, vary from moment to moment. Not infrequently, for instance, it seems that the intensity of directional activity is maximal at the very time when one actone is being replaced by another (*cf.* violent trial and error movements).

10. An investigator may often interrupt the action pattern of his subject by bringing about the appropriate effect (the "goal" of the subject) himself. This may be termed a *gratuity*, or gratuitous end situation. According to the need theory this should relieve the need tension and, as it usually does, stop the action. But if the actone itself were the dynamic factor, the presentation of the E.S. would not interrupt it. The actone would continue to its completion.

11. That a need is an important determinant of certain kinds of behaviour is shown by the fact that when it is neither active nor in a state of readiness responses to specific stimuli do not occur.

(*a*) Animals recently fed do not commonly respond to food.

(*b*) Female guinea pigs exhibit the copulatory reflex only during oestrous.

12. When a particular need is active, common objects in the environment may evoke uncommon responses—responses which promote the progress of the active need. Thus, the usual *S-R* connections may not be exhibited.

When a boy, who is quarrelling with a playmate, sees an apple, he may not respond, as he usually does, by eating it, but, instead, may throw it at his antagonist.

It seems highly probable that many of the S-R connections which are considered stable by experimenters are stable only under the conditions of their experiments, that is, when the same need—usually hunger—is active in the organism.

13. When a need becomes active a characteristic trend of behaviour will usually ensue even in the absence of the customary stimuli.

An animal will *explore* for food, and a man will *search* for a sex object.

14. Difficult to interpret without a concept of directional tension are the following: the *resumption* of unpleasant work after interruption (*cf.* Lewin), the repetition of once-active trends with different movements, the *increase* of striving after opposition.

15. Positivists are usually disinclined to accept the concept of drive, because they cannot, as it were, get their hands on it. It seems like a vague, airy conception —perhaps a disguised emissary of theology and metaphysics. That some day definite *sources* of the drives may be discovered is suggested by certain recent findings, and these constitute another argument in favor of the concept.

(*a*) The recent researches of Riddle (4) indicate that prolactin—a pituitary hormone—is responsible for the nurturing, or parental activity of rats. (*b*) The findings of Young[2] show that two secretions—the luteinizing hormone from the pituitary and progesterol from the ovary—bring on oestrous in guinea pigs.

Up to this point the evidence in support of the concept of internal driving forces has been derived from extrospection. I have presented only external public and objective facts. I shall now, without shame, turn to the testimony offered by internal private and subjective facts, including a few additional objective facts for full measure.

16. Introspection has given us a good deal of informa-

[2] Young, W. C., paper presented at the Harvard Psychological Colloquium, April 22, 1936, "The hormonal production of sexual receptivity in the guinea pig."

tion about the subjective entities that are necessary for the formulation of mental, and, hence, we must suppose, of cortical events. If the double aspect theory—which seems to be the best available hypothesis—is approximately correct, every subjective entity must have a physical correlate. Consequently, we should expect to find a cortical or sub-cortical process co-existing with the experiences of desiring (volition, conation, *etc.*). Since a need, as defined, closely resembles in all its relations, the inner feeling of tension which makes us strive to attain a certain goal, we may tentatively suppose that a need is an electro-chemical process of some sort which is inwardly felt as the force of desire.

> The subjective experiences of desiring, intending, or planning commonly precedes the experience of striving. It is, therefore, pre-motor, just as a need, by definition, is pre-motor.
>
> Since a need is commonly aroused by certain afferent processes and since it may justly be considered the physical correlate of the force of desire, and since, finally, as we shall see, it directly affects perception and thought, we may tentatively suppose that it is located in the brain—"between" the sensory and motor areas. It is, let us say, a directional tension (one might almost say a facilitation) which is the resultant of certain electrical or chemical processes originating in other, more or less specific, parts of the body. This, of course—is highly speculative.

If we assume, then, that desire and drive are two aspects of the same thing, we may use introspection to reveal to us some of the possible internal relations of drives. For instance, it is reasonable to suppose, as objective researches (*cf.* Tolman) and introspection suggest, that every need is associated with traces (or images) representing movements, pathways, agencies and goal objects, which, taken together, constitute a *need integrate*. This need integrate is in the nature of a fantasy which depicts a possible trend of events. Hence, from now on when we speak of a drive it will be convenient to think of a force in the brain propelling a flow of images—images which refer, for the most part, to objects once perceived in conjunction with the activity of the same drive. With this in mind, we may consider a num-

ber of other facts, mostly subjective, which seem to call
for a concept of directional tensions in the brain region.

17. Among the commonest subjective experiences is
that of conflict between desires, and that of one desire
inhibiting another. If psychology limits itself to concepts
which refer only to external movements, there will be no
way of formulating important psychological events of
this kind.

> Inner conflicts between alternate mechanisms are less im-
> portant than those between alternate needs—such, let us say,
> as a conflict between the desire to injure a man and the
> desire to avoid censure.

18. Although many psychologists may describe events
without explicit mention of affection (pleasure or unpleasure) they are unable to get along without this variable when they have to deal practically with themselves
or with others. I might even suggest that the problem
of what determines happiness is as important as any in
psychology. This is not the time to discuss hedonism,
but I may say, at least, what most people, I think, would
agree to, namely, that pleasure is closely associated with
a successful trend—the moving towards and final
achievement of a major effect. It is less closely associated
with activity *qua activity*—movements, let us say, which
achieve nothing. Furthermore, introspection seems to reveal that a need does not cease (is not "satisfied") until
pleasure is experienced. In fact, it often happens that we
do not properly distinguish a need until an object that
brings pleasure informs us of what it was we wanted. The
point that I am making here is this: that because of its
close connection with happiness and distress, a need is
more "important" than an action pattern.

19. Experience seems to show that a certain desire
may sometimes give rise to a dream or fantasy and at
other times promote overt activity. Without the concept
of an underlying drive one could not adequately represent the obvious relationship between fantasy and behaviour.

> There is a good deal of evidence to support the view that
> under certain conditions fantasy may partially relieve the

tension of a need. That is, it may be the equivalent of overt action.

20. Introspection and experiment demonstrate that a need or an emotion may determine the direction of attention and markedly influence the perception and apperception (interpretation) of external occurrences. To influence sensory and cognitive processes a need must be some force in the brain region.

(a) Sanford (5) has shown that hunger will influence a child's completion of unfinished pictures. (b) Murray (3) has shown that fear will change a child's interpretation of photographs.

21. Experience seems to show that sentiments and theories are also to some extent determined by desires. A man likes and tries to prove the value of what he wants. He also "projects" his own needs into his psychological theories.

22. Introspection and clinical observation reveal that different desires (or trends) may be related in a variety of ways: one form of behaviour may satisfy two or more desires, a desire may inhibit another, one trend may serve to finally promote another, a trend may be succeeded by its opposite (ambitendency), etc. Such relationship cannot be formulated without a concept of different directional processes interacting in one region of the body, the brain.

23. Without a concept of motivating forces most of the phenomena of abnormal psychology would be wholly unintelligible—compulsion, conflict, repression, conversion, displacement, sublimation, delusion and so forth. And without such a concept a therapist would be literally tongue-tied. He would communicate neither with his patient nor with his colleagues.

When we consider that no therapeutist or, indeed, anyone who has to deal in a practical way with human beings, can get along without some notion of motivational force (instinct, need, drive, impulse, urge, inclination, wish, desire, or what not), the suspicion naturally arises that those who entertain a prejudice against such a concept do so on metaphysical or "religious" grounds.

GENERAL CONSIDERATIONS

In so far as a need is defined as a disequilibrium which stresses towards equilibrium, it falls into the category of finalistic concepts, of which the Second Law of Thermodynamics is typical. The latter has been stated as follows: "In all processes with which we are acquainted, every known form of energy at a high potential always tends to run down to energy at the lowest potential circumstances will allow." According to this principle affairs tend to take a certain course. The need concept affirms this and no more.

The fundamental hypothesis is that an active need tends to propel thought and action in a certain direction. The immediate cause of the behaviour is the existing tension, and this tension, in turn, is the resultant of afferent excitations as well as of the fluid conditions—chemical constitution of blood and lymph—in the brain region. It is the lowering of specific tensions which may be regarded as the general "purpose" of behaviour. A need is clearly an emergence from the past, or, as Schopenhauer would have it, "a push from the rear," rather than an incentive or "pull from the future." Imaginal representations of the goal (conscious purpose) may or may not occur. To put it metaphorically, a need may have no inkling of *what* it needs. It may be blind impulse, but impulse which does not completely subside until a situation of a certain kind has been arrived at. It is because of this that we speak of drive as a finalistic rather than a mechanistic concept. Those who use finalism in some other sense should not apply it to the need theory as here developed.

This, of course, does not supersede the mechanistic account of things. For we must also take cognizance of the stimulus-response sequences, the linked actones and agencies by means of which the closing situation is achieved and the tension lowered. "The fact is," as L. J. Henderson has put it, "there is both mechanism and finalism in nature." To psychologists who bristle when "purpose" is mentioned, I am tempted to quote Whitehead: "Scientists animated by the purpose of proving that

they are purposeless constitute an interesting subject
for study."

From this exposition it should be clear that the term
"need" or "drive" does not denote an observable fact—
the direction of activity, for example. For this we have
the terms "behavioural trend" or "behavioural effect."
Nor does "drive" refer to any attribute of general activity
as such. It refers to a hypothetical process within the brain
of an organism which, perseverating for a time, "points"
activity and coordinates it. If opposed by another need
process, however, it may not manifest itself overtly.

Again, it should be clear that the term "need" or
"drive" does not stand for any physiological occurrences
(visceral tension or endocrine secretion) which may lead
up to or evoke the directive processes in the brain. The
former may be termed "sources" or "provokers" of needs,
but they are not themselves need processes. A hormone, for instance, is not the same thing as the cephalic
process (the subjective aspect of which is a "wish") to
which it may give rise; and the latter should be differentiated from the observed trend of behaviour. The need is
"placed" in the brain, because it is the regnant processes
in this region which we, as psychologists, must ultimately
attempt to formulate. If we do not, we shall never bring
together into one conceptual scheme the facts of behaviour, the facts of brain physiology and pathology, and
the facts of consciousness. It does not seem possible to
place the factor which determines the directional effective-
ness or intensity of behaviour either in the afferent or in
the efferent systems. It must be post-afferent and pre-
efferent. The fact that we cannot conjure up an image
of what such a cephalic field force might resemble is no
reason for hesitating to use the concept as a working
hypothesis.

In the present article the attempt has been made to
assemble facts—objective and subjective—which seem to
call for a concept of drive or need. The approach differs
from that adopted by the psychologists who "state," "af-
firm" or "assert" that organisms are so constituted that
they "seek or strive for certain natural goals." We did
not start with an assertion. We merely pointed out that
an hypothesis of a driving force helps to order some of

the facts. According to this view a need is not a reified entity extrinsic to the system. It stands for the momentary direction of regnant processes in the brain region. It is always in a state of mutual dependence with the other cephalic forces. It may change from one split second to the next. To say that an organism has a certain drive—let us say, a sex drive—when that drive is not at the moment active, is to make a very abstract, though convenient, statement. Such an assertion actually means that a certain trend has commonly occurred in the past and, if conditions are suitable, it may recur in the future.

Instinct, the noun, is a word to be avoided, because it has been extensively used in two different senses: to signify innate actones and to signify innate needs.

> "It is true that if we consider the structure of the action pattern only, disregarding for the time being its origin, we cannot easily distinguish instinct from habit, for both are in their pure form, automatic stimulus-response processes" [Bernard (1)]
>
> "It is not the details of the response that are fixed by the innate factor we have called instinct, but rather the general nature of the end towards which the response shall move; the details are fixed by the limitations of the creature's intelligence and the structure of its sensory-motor mechanism" [Garnett (2)].

Since behaviour is an important part of personality the science of personology cannot advance much further without a classification of the more important trends of behaviour, or needs. In constructing such a classification, however, it is not necessary to limit oneself to needs which appear to be inherited. Which of the needs are innate, and to what extent, is another question—one for further observation and experiment.

REFERENCES

1. BERNARD, L. L. *Instincts*. New York: Henry Holt, 1924. Pp. ix+550.
2. GARNETT, A. C. *The Mind in Action*. New York: D. Appleton, 1931. Pp. 218.
3. MURRAY, H. A. The effect of fear upon estimates of the maliciousness of other personalities. *J. Soc. Psychol.*, 1933, 4, 310-339.

4. RIDDLE, O., LAHR, E. L., & BATES, R. W. Maternal behavior induced in rats by prolactin. *Proc. Soc. Exper. Biol.*, New York, 1935, 32, 730-734.
5. SANFORD, R. N. The effects of abstinence from food upon imaginal processes: A preliminary experiment. *J. Psychol.*, 1936, 2, 129-136.
6. SKINNER, B. F. The generic nature of the concepts of stimulus and response. *J. Gen. Psychol.*, 1935, 12, 40-65.

5

Toward a Theory of Motivation

DAVID C. MCCLELLAND, *Harvard University*
JOHN W. ATKINSON, *University of Michigan*
RUSSELL A. CLARK, *University of Michigan*
EDGAR L. LOWELL, *Harvard University*

The affective arousal model. Our reservations with respect to contemporary motivation theory have led us to attempt to rough out proposals for an alternative theory which may now or ultimately meet some of these objections and handle the data at least as well as the other models discussed. We are well aware of the incompleteness, as of this writing, of our theoretical thinking, but we will attempt to state our views as precisely and forcefully as we can in the hope that we can stimulate more serious discussion and experimental testing of motivational theory. At several points we will be obliged to present alternative hypotheses, since we do not as yet have the data to decide between them. But we agree with Hull and others that the only way to make progress in a field is "to stick one's neck out" and to state implicit theoretical assumptions as explicitly as possible.

Our definition of a motive is this: *A motive is the redintegration by a cue of a change in an affective situation.* The word *redintegration* in this definition is meant to imply previous learning. In our system, all motives are learned. The basic idea is simply this: Certain stimuli or situations involving discrepancies between expectation (adaptation level) and perception are sources of primary, unlearned affect, either positive or negative in nature. Cues which are paired with these affective states, changes in these affective states, and the conditions producing them become capable of redintegrating a state (A') derived from the original affective situation (A), but not identical with it. To give a simple example, this means that if a buzzer is associated with eating saccharine the buzzer will in time attain the power to evoke a motive or redintegrate a state involving positive affective change. Likewise, the buzzer if associated with shock will achieve the power to redintegrate a negative affective state. These redintegrated states, which might be called respectively *appetite* and *anxiety*, are based on the primary affective situation but are not identical with it.

The term *change in affect* is used in two separate senses. It refers on the one hand to the fact that *at the time of arousal* of a motive, the affective state which is redintegrated must be different from the one already experienced by the organism, and on the other hand to the *possibility* that *at the time of acquisition* of a motive, the affective state with which the cue gets associated must be undergoing a change. We are agreed that a "change in affect" at the time of arousal in the first sense must occur, but we see two possibilities on the acquisition side of the picture—one, that the association is with a *static* affective state; the other, that it is with a *changing* affective state. To elaborate this point further, the first alternative states simply that any cue associated with a situation producing affect will acquire the power to evoke a "model" of that situation (A') which will serve as a motive. The second alternative requires that the cue be associated with a *changing* state—of going from "shock" to "no shock" or from neutrality to pleasure, and so forth. The difference between the two possibilities is illustrated in the following diagram:

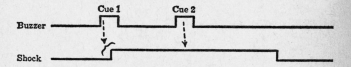

According to the first hypothesis, both cue 1 and cue 2 should be capable of evoking an avoidance motive, since they have both been paired with the affective state arising from shock. According to the second, alternative hypothesis, cue 2 should have weak or nonexistent motivating power since it has not been associated with a *change*

in affect. It should be possible to determine which of these alternatives is correct by experimentation along these lines. Finally, it should be repeated that both hypotheses assume that the redintegrated affect *at the time of arousal* must represent a change over the present affective state of the organism.

In the discussion so far there has been some ambiguity as to just what is redintegrated—the affective state or change, the conditions which produced it, or both. Actually, the ambiguity reflects some uncertainty as to which alternative is correct and also some difficulty in expressing simply exactly what happens. By far the most likely possibility is that both the situation *and* the affect it produces are redintegrated. Thus the redintegrated "situation" defines the goal in the usual sense (e.g., sugar in the mouth), and the redintegrated "affect" (e.g., reaction to the sugar in the mouth) determines whether the goal is motivating or not. For the sake of simplicity, phrases like redintegrated "affective state" or "affective change" are used throughout this chapter to refer both to the affective reaction itself and the situation which produced it.

Two main questions connected with the concept of redintegrated affective state still remain to be answered. Why, first of all, should we have decided to base motives on affect? Secondly, how are we to determine the existence of affective arousal? It will be difficult to do complete justice to these questions, but a word on each may help indicate the progress of our thinking.

2.8 *Why affect as a basis for motives?* We have decided to base motives on affective arousal, following Young's lead (1949) for several reasons. In the first place, it seems apparent that the motive concept will be useful only if it has some kind of a limited base. That is, if all associations are motivating, then there seems no particular reason to introduce the concept of motivation to apply to a particular sub-class of association. Thus the associations involved in forming motives must be in some way different from other types of associations. And we have chosen affective states as the basis for motives rather than biological needs or strong stimuli because of the limitations of those concepts already discussed. A more positive reason for choosing affective states as primary is that they are "obviously" important in controlling behavior, at least at the common-sense level. The hedonic or pleasure-pain view of motivation is certainly one of the oldest in psychological thinking and can be traced at least to Plato's *Protagoras*. Furthermore, in order to get motives in the laboratory we commonly pair cues with affective states resulting from shock, saccharine in the mouth, food deprivation, and the like. Operationally we manipulate states which we know subjectively will produce pleasure and pain when we work with motives.

Another reason for choosing affect as the basis for motives rather than tissue needs, etc., is the overwhelming evidence for the importance of selective sensitivity in guiding and directing behavior in lower animals. Tinbergen (1951) has collected dozens of cases which illustrate how special stimuli are required to release a particular "consummatory" response particularly in submammalian species. Young (1949) has repeatedly called attention to the different palatability of various foods for the white rat. Weiner and Stellar (1951) have demonstrated unlearned salt preferences in the rat. And so forth. The list could easily be extended. The usual reaction by theorists to these facts is to assume that they are not characteristic of the human animal, which is obviously much more dependent on learning than on innate reactions to particular "releasing" stimuli. The difference is nicely highlighted by Ford and Beach (1951), who show how human sexual behavior is much less dependent than the behavior of lower animals on particular external signs and internal hormonal conditions.

But all of this seems no reason to assume a sharp discontinuity between man and other animals with respect to the factors controlling behavior. Rather we have been struck by the possibility that man's behavior may also be guided by selective sensitivity to particular kinds of situations. The difference may be one of degree rather than kind. With man the "releasing" situations may be much less specific than the dot on a gull's beak which releases pecking behavior of a gull chick, but they may exist just the same (Section 2.10). And the consummatory reactions elicited by such situations may also be much less specific and rigid than the pecking, fighting, courting responses shown in lower animals; in fact, the interesting possibility pursued here is that in man these specific overt reactions to "releasing" stimuli are attenuated and occur instead as diffuse reactions of the autonomic nervous system signifying what we usually call "affect." Thus our motivational system for man has been constructed to parallel the analysis of instinctive behavior in lower animals made by Tinbergen (1951) and others. Certain types of situations (Section 2.10) innately release reactions which are diffuse and covert in man rather than specific and overt, but which are consummatory in the same sense in that they ultimately exhaust themselves. These diffuse reactions are what we mean by affect, and they can be observed either through verbal reports and autonomic reactions, or inferred from approach and avoidance behavior, as we shall see in the next section. Man's advantage over lower animals lies precisely in the wider range of situations which will produce affect and in the lack of overt specificity of the affective reaction. Thus he can build a wide variety of motives on a much broader base, but to our mind it is essentially the same base as that which is responsible for guiding and directing the behavior of lower animals.

2.9 *Behavioral effects of affective arousal.* But how do we propose to define pleasure and pain or affective arousal? We certainly do not intend to fall into the trap of arguing that pleasurable sensations are those that lead to survival, and painful ones those that ultimately lead to maladaptation and death. This answer lands us back in the same difficulties that face the biological need theory of motivation. Let us first attempt to define affect by anchoring it on the behavioral side. It might seem more logical to consider first the antecedent conditions of affect (see Section 2.10) rather than its behavioral consequences, but the behavioral approach is more familiar because it is the one that has been customarily employed in attempts to measure affect or pleasure and pain (cf. Lindsley in Stevens, 1951). Thus, at a certain gross level, one can distinguish affective states from other states by the effects of autonomic activity—changes in respiration rate, in electrical skin resistance, in blood pressure, and the like. Thus one might initially state as a generalization that an affective state is present whenever the *PGR* shows a significant deflection, and that anyone who wants to establish a motive can simply pair cues with such deflections or the conditions which produced them. Autonomic accompaniments of emotions may not be perfect indexes of their presence, but they are sufficiently good to provide a very practical basis for deciding in a large number of cases that affective arousal has occurred.

Since autonomic measures apparently cannot be used at the present time to distinguish sensitively between positive and negative affective states, we will need to attack this problem in some other way. There are several possibilities. Among humans, expressive movements can readily be interpreted as indicating pleasant or unpleasant feeling states, particularly facial expressions (Schlosberg, 1952). Impromptu vocalizing seems also to be a good indicator of mood. Probably the most sensitive and frequently used index to hedonic tone is verbal behavior. If the person says "I dislike it," "I'm unhappy," or "it hurts," we take it as a sign of negative affect. If he says "I feel good," or "I like it," we take it as a sign of positive affect. One difficulty with these expressive signs is that they are not infallible. They can all be "faked," or changed by learning.

And what about animals? They can't talk, it would be difficult to try to interpret the facial expression of a rat or an elephant, and no one has made a careful study of animal vocalization patterns in response to pleasure and pain. In the case of some animals, certain innate response patterns are readily interpreted as signifying positive or negative affect—e.g., purring or spitting in the cat; licking, tail-wagging, or growling in the dog, and so on. More attention should be given to the study of the expressive signs of affect, but until it is, we must be satisfied with stopgap measures. Probably the most useful of these with adult animals is simple preference or approach behavior in contrast to avoidance behavior.

Sometimes there are reflex responses that are clearly approach or avoidance in nature—e.g., sucking, grasping, swallowing, spitting, vomiting, blinking—and in some instances they may provide direct evidence of positive or negative affective arousal. That is, eye-blinking in response to a puff of air, if accompanied by an autonomic response, would give evidence that affect was present and that this affect was negative in nature. Cues paired with the air puff would in time come to elicit an avoidance motive (as indicated by the presence of an avoidance *response*—the conditional or anticipatory eye-blink). But since reflexes are few in number and sometimes hard to classify as approach or avoidance (e.g., the knee jerk), better evidence for the existence of affective arousal is to be found in *learned* approach and avoidance behavior (locomotor, manual, verbal). There is an apparent circularity here, because what we are saying is that we can tell whether affective arousal occurred only after the organism has learned an approach or avoidance response in the service of a motive. Are we not first making a motive dependent on affective arousal and then saying we can find out whether affective arousal occurred if a motive has been formed which leads to approach or avoidance behavior? The answer is "Yes, we are," but the argument is not completely circular (cf. Meehl, 1950). Thus in one experiment we can determine that salty water leads to learned approach or preference behavior in the rat and we can then *infer* from this that it produces positive affective arousal. This inference (that salty water "tastes good" to the rat) can then be used as the basis for new learning experiments, theorizing, and so on. In this way we can gradually build up classes of objects, situations, response categories, or sensations which must produce affective arousal and then try to generalize as to what they have in common, as we have later on in this chapter (Section 2.10). In brief, the notion here is to use autonomic responses to indicate the presence of affect and approach and avoidance (either learned or reflex) to distinguish positive from negative affect.

There is one misconception which may arise in connection with this definition that it is well to anticipate, however. The terms *approach* and *avoidance* must not be understood simply as "going towards" or "away from" a stimulus in a spatial sense. Thus "rage," when it goes over into attack, is an "avoidance" response, even though it involves "going towards" something. *Avoidance* must be defined in terms of its objective—to discontinue, remove, or escape from a certain type of stimulation and not in terms of its overt characteristics. Attack has, as its objective, removal of the source of stimulation in the same sense that withdrawal does. *Approach* must also be defined functionally—i.e., it is any activity, the objective of which is to continue, maintain, or pursue a certain kind of stimulation. Because of the ambiguity involved in using these terms, it might be better to substitute others like *stimulus enhancement* or *stimulus reduction*, but approach and avoidance have the advantage of common usage and if it is understood that they are used in a functional sense, difficulties should not arise in using them as the primary means of defining positive and negative affect on the response side. It is perhaps worth noting that Dearborn (1899) and Corwin (1921) came to the same decision long ago after recording involuntary "pursuit" (extension) and "withdrawal" (flexion) movements to pleasant and unpleasant stimuli, respectively.

2.9.1 *Distinguishing the effects of affect and motive.* Analytically speaking, there are three events involved in the development of a motive, any of which may have observable and distinguishable behavioral effects. In order of occurrence, they are:

A. The situation producing affect
B. Redintegration of (A)
C. Response learned to (B)

We have discussed the problem of measuring the behavorial effects of A in the previous section. How can the effects of A and B be distinguished, if at all? The simplest assumption would seem to be the one that Hull made years ago (1931), to the effect that a cue paired with a goal response will evoke a fractional anticipatory portion of it. The notion behind this is that the redintegrated response is like the original but fractional in nature, that is, consisting of a portion of the total goal response which is perhaps less in intensity or duration. The difficulty with this idea has been discussed at some length by Mowrer (1950). In general, the objection is similar to the one made against the substitution hypothesis in conditioning experiments. That is, formerly it was commonly assumed that in conditioning the conditioned stimulus simply substituted for the unconditioned stimulus in evoking the unconditioned response. But, as Hilgard and Marquis (1940) point out, the conditioned response is in fact often quite different from the unconditioned response. It is not necessarily a miniature replica or fractional portion of the original unconditioned response. For example, there is evidence that the normal response in rats to the primary affective state produced by shock is squealing, defecating, and intense variable behavior, whereas the normal response to anticipation of shock (e.g., to fear) is different, probably crouching (Arnold, 1945). The evidence that crouching is the normal response to fear is not conclusive, as Brown and Jacobs (1949) point out, because it can be eliminated by certain experimental procedures; but the probability is still fairly great that the response to fear differs in important ways from the response to shock. Therefore it would seem unwise at this state of our knowledge to assume that the fear response is just a partial copy of the shock response. At the phenomenological level, it seems that shock produces two distinguishable response elements—pain, which is the immediate reaction to shock, and fear, which is the anticipatory redintegration of the pain response. These two responses are clearly different. That is, if one's teeth are hurt by drilling in the dentist's chair, the sight of the chair may evoke a subjective feeling we label fear, but it does not evoke a "fractional" pain in the teeth.

When we consider the third event in the sequence of motive formation—namely, the responses learned to the redintegrated affect—the picture becomes even more complex. Our position is that the genotypic responses to redintegrated positive or negative affect are "functional" approach or avoidance. Thus from avoidance we can infer that negative affect has occurred if we lack a direct independent response definition of negative affect. But at the phenotypical level, the responses learned to redintegrated negative or positive affect may be very varied. A rat can be trained to run at as well as away from a shock (Gwinn, 1949). Rage and fear are genotypically avoidance responses, but phenotypically the former involves approach and the latter withdrawal. Similarly, love and contempt or scorn are genotypically similar in that they both involve attempts to maintain a source of stimulation, but phenotypically love involves "going towards" an object and scorn involves "keeping your distance" from the scorned object. A classification of emotions on a pleasant-unpleasant dimension and on an attentive-rejective one succeeds in ordering satisfactorily nearly all the facial expressions of emotion, according to Schlosberg (1952), a fact which tends to confirm our position that one must distinguish basically between positive and negative affect on the one hand and learned reactions to it, however classified, on the other. If the learned reactions are classified as to whether they phenotypically involve "going towards" or "away from" something, as they were approximately on Schlosberg's attentive-rejective dimension, then one gets a fourfold table in which Love, Contempt, Rage, and Fear represent the four major types of emotional reactions.

But obviously such classifications of phenotypic reactions can vary tremendously. The important points to keep in mind theoretically are (1) that they are surface modes of reaction with two basic objectives—to approach or maintain pleasure and to avoid or reduce pain, and (2) that they are acquired and hence take time to develop and show characteristic individual differences.

2.10 *Antecedent conditions for affective arousal.* Let us now focus our attention on the all-important problem of identifying the antecedent conditions which produce affective arousal. For if we know them, we are in a position, according to the theory, of knowing how to create a motive by pairing cues with those conditions. . . . Considering the antecedent conditions for affective arousal inevitably gets us into some ancient controversies over what causes pleasure and pain (McDougall, 1927; Beebe-Center, 1932; Dallenbach, 1939; Hebb, 1949). There is not the space here to review these controversies or to attempt to resolve them. Instead, we can only indicate what appears to us to be a promising approach to a general theory. This approach can only be outlined roughly here in the form of a series of propositions which seem promising to us but which will require experimentation and more detailed exposition in further publications.*

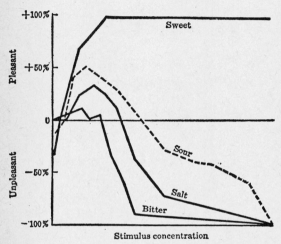

Fig. 1. *Preponderance of "pleasant" or "unpleasant" judgments in relation to the concentration of a sapid solution. The ordinate gives per cent "pleasant" minus per cent "unpleasant." The abscissa is proportional to the concentration, the full length of the baseline standing for 40 per cent cane sugar, for 10 per cent salt, and for .004 per cent quinine sulphate (all by weight). Data of R. Engel, after Woodworth, 1938.*

2.10.1 *Affective arousal is the innate consequence of certain sensory or perceptual events.* It is probable (though not necessary) that the basic mechanism (see proposition 2) which gives rise to *sensory* pleasantness (e.g., sweetness) and unpleasantness (e.g., bitterness) is similar to that which gives rise to pleasantness-unpleas-

* D.C.McC. and R.A.C. are largely responsible for Section 2.10, which was written after the main body of the text had been completed.

antness at a more complex perceptual level (pleasant music vs. dissonant music). In this connection we use the term *sensory* to refer roughly to simple variations in stimulus dimensions (e.g., stimulus intensity), whereas *perceptual* refers primarily to more complex variations in stimulus events.

2.10.2 *Positive affect is the result of smaller discrepancies of a sensory or perceptual event from the adaptation level of the organism; negative affect is the result of larger discrepancies.* The salt curve in Figure 1 illustrates this postulated relationship from the hedonic reactions to increasing salt concentrations in the mouth. Fifty years ago it was a commonplace assumption that increasing sensory intensity in *any* modality produced a pleasantness-unpleasantness curve like this (Beebe-Center, 1932, p. 166). The new feature of such a curve for us is that, like Hebb, we would plot it not against increasing intensity as such but against size of discrepancy between the stimulus (perception) and the adaptation level of the organism (expectation). Such a modification has several advantages which we will enumerate, but among them is the fact that it brings the "discrepancy hypothesis" as to the source of affect within the realm of quantitative testing according to Helson's formulae (1948) for determining adaptation level and discrepancies from it. In the discussion which follows we have obviously leaned heavily on Helson's formulation of the concept of adaptation level.

2.10.3 *Natural adaptation levels for various sensory receptors differ.* Such a hypothesis is apparently essential to a discrepancy hypothesis because of the known fact that some receptors give rise most readily or "naturally" to pleasantness and others to unpleasantness. In Figure 1 the two curves for sweet and bitter sensations illustrate this point. Thus sugar appears to give rise to pleasurable sensations across the entire range of stimulus intensity. In terms of the discrepancy hypothesis, this suggests that a discrepancy from the natural adaptation level (*AL*) large enough to produce unpleasantness is not possible. The bitter curve, on the other hand, is quite different: here nearly all intensities of stimulus concentration tested give rise to negative affect. The fact that the absolute threshold for sugar is considerably above what it is for bitter (Pfaffman in Stevens, 1951) suggests the following interpretation. The threshold for sweet is relatively high and the range of stimulation to which it is sensitive sufficiently narrow so that large discrepancies from AL which probably lies near the threshold are impossible. With bitter the threshold is so low that small fractions of the maximum concentration used in Figure 1 still represent fairly large discrepancies from an AL near the threshold. At this stage of our knowledge easy generalizations must be avoided, but it seems obvious even now that ultimately the natural AL for a receptor will turn out to be somewhere near its threshold (modified perhaps by the normal stimulation impinging on it) and that the size of the discrepancies which will yield positive and negative affect will be a joint rational function of the three constants in receptor functioning—the lower threshold, the upper threshold, and the Weber fraction.

REFERENCES

ARNOLD, MAGDA B., Physiological differentiation of emotional states. *Psychol. Rev.*, 1945, p. 36.

BEEBE-CENTER, J. G., *The psychology of pleasantness and unpleasantness*. New York: Van Nostrand, 1932, pp. 42, 44, 52 & 64.

BROWN, J. S., and JACOBS, A., The role of fear in the motivation and acquisition of responses. *J. exp. Psychol.*, 1949, 39, p. 36.

CORWIN, G. H., The involuntary response to unpleasantness. *Amer. J. Psychol.*, 1921, 32, p. 35.

DALLENBACH, K. M., Pain: history and present status. *Amer. J. Psychol.*, 1939, 52, p. 42.

DEARBORN, G. V. N., The emotion of joy. *Psychol. Rev.* (Monogr. Suppl.) 1899, 2, no. 5, p. 35.

FORD, C. S. and BEACH, F. A. *Patterns of sexual behavior.* New York: Harper, 1951, p. 31.

GWINN, G. T., The effects of punishment on acts motivated by fear. *J. exp. Psychol.*, 1949, 39, p. 37.

HEBB, D. O., *The organization of behavior*. New York: Wiley, 1949, pp. 42, 48 & 60.

HELSON, H., Adaptation-level as a basis for a quantitative theory of frames of reference. *Psychol. Rev.*, 1948, 55, pp. 44 & 58.

HILGARD, E. R. and MARQUIS, D. G., *Conditioning and learning*. New York: Appleton-Century-Crofts, 1940, p. 36.

HULL, C. L., Goal attraction and direction ideas conceived as habit phenomena. *Psychol. Rev.*, 1931, p. 36.

LINDSLEY, D. B., Emotion. in S. S. Stevens (ed.), *Handbook of experimental psychology.* New York: John Wiley & Sons, Inc., 1951, p. 32.

McDOUGALL, W., Pleasure, pain and conation. *Brit. J. Psychol.*, 1927, 17, p. 42.

MEEHL, P. E., On the circularity of the law of effect. *Psychol. Bull.*, 1950, 47, p. 34.

MOWRER, O. H., *Learning theory and personality dynamics*. New York: Ronald Press, 1950, p. 36.

PFAFFMAN, C., Taste and smell. in S. S. Stevens (ed.), *Handbook of experimental psychology*. New York: John Wiley & Sons, Inc., 1951, p. 44.

SCHLOSBERG, H., The description of facial expressions in terms of two dimensions. *J. exp. Psychol.*, 1952, 44, pp. 33 & 37.

TINBERGEN, N., *The study of instinct*. London: Oxford, Clarendon Press, 1951, pp. 31 & 32.

WEINER, I. H., and STELLAR, E., Salt preference of the rat determined by a single stimulus method. *J. comp. physiol. psychol.*, 1951, 44, p. 31.

YOUNG, P. T., Food-seeking drive, affective processes, and learning. *Psychol. Rev.*, 1949, 56, pp. 31 & 32.

6

Deficiency Motivation and Growth Motivation

ABRAHAM MASLOW
Brandeis University

Hans Zinsser has described the difference between philosophical and scientific theorizing by comparing the latter to a trellis which one builds out just ahead of the growing vine in the direction of its growth and for the sake of its future support. It is this latter task that I have set myself in this paper which is a portion of a larger systematic theory of general psychology. It is based mostly upon clinical and personological researches and experience, rather than upon formal experimentation but will soon be ready, I think, for the experimental test. I must warn you that the demands of system and of theory probably play a considerable role in what follows. To some extent, its existence and its particular shape are called for not only by data but also by theoretical, systematic considerations of which I cannot speak here, and which will be apparent only when the whole structure of theory is seen as a unity.

Another point that I must warn you about is this. This paper is very frankly in a different tradition from the ones you have heard in previous years in this series. For one thing, I am not *only* the disinterested and impersonal seeker for pure cold truth for its own sake. I am also very definitely interested and concerned with man's fate, with his ends and goals and with his future. I would like to help improve him and to better his prospects. I

Reprinted from *The Nebraska Symposium* edited by Marshall R. Jones, University of Nebraska Press, 1955, with permission of the author and publishers.

hope to help teach him how to be brotherly, cooperative, peaceful, courageous and just. I think science is the best hope for achieving this, and of all the sciences I consider psychology the most important to this end. Indeed I sometimes think that the world will either be saved by psychologists—in the very broadest sense—or else it will not be saved at all. It is this humanistic emphasis which is the source and the justification of what I consider to be the important questions which justify inexact and unreliable researches. They *must* be done; we don't *dare* turn away from them because we can't handle them well. We must do the best we can.

Psychology as a science in the United States has considered itself to stand in a line stemming primarily from Wundt and the German experimental psychology (neglecting by the way the French tradition which is quite different and to my taste far more fruitful). I remind you, with Fromm, that we have forgotten in this country another line of development and another time-honored task for psychology. Aristotle, Spinoza, James, Goldstein, G. Allport, and Fromm are a few of the names in this tradition that considers the humanistic task of psychology to be that of constructing a scientific system of values to help men live the good life, i.e., a humanly usable theory of human motivation.

Few papers in this series up to the present have derived ultimately from psychoanalytic sources. This is a serious lack since it is the opinion of all but a few that in spite of many mistakes and false leads, the various schools of psychoanalysis have contributed more to the understanding of human motivation than all other sources combined throughout human history. This is true not only for profound questions raised and bold hypotheses offered, but also for research methods and findings. I believe that there are empirical methods other than the experimental. There *must* be, even *a priori*, for experimentation is generally the *last* step in the acquisition of knowledge rather than the first. Much theorizing and naturalistic observing has to be done before worthwhile experiments are possible. The experimenter is the last member of a relay team.

To think otherwise is to be parochial and puffed up with scientific pride. Hubris can be a scientific sin too. Psychologists (who tend to demand that every baby should be born with a full set of teeth) must learn to turn humbly to USE any source of information, however inchoate, unformed and embryonic it may be.

The concept "basic need" can be defined in terms of the questions which it answers and the operations which uncovered it. My original question was about psycho-pathogenesis. "What makes people neurotic?" My an-swer (a modification of and I think an improvement upon the analytic one) was, in brief, that neurosis seemed at its core, and in its beginning, to be a deficiency dis-ease; that it was born out of being deprived of certain satisfactions which I called needs in the same sense that water and amino acids and calcium are needs, namely that their absence produces illness. Most neuroses in-volved, along with other complex determinants, ungrati-fied wishes for safety, for belongingness and identification, for close love relationships and for respect and prestige. My "data" were gathered through twelve years of psy-chotherapeutic work and research and twenty years of personality study. One obvious control research (done at the same time and in the same operation) was on the effect of replacement therapy which showed, with many complexities, that when these deficiencies were elimi-nated, sicknesses tended to disappear. Still another neces-sary long-time control research was on the family back-grounds of both neurotic and healthy people establishing, as many others have since done, that people who are later healthy are not deprived of these essential basic-need-satisfactions, i.e., the prophylactic control.

These conclusions, which are now in effect shared by most clinicians, therapists, and child psychologists (many of them would not phrase it as I have) make it more possible year by year to define need, in a natural, easy spontaneous way, as a generalization of actual experi-ential data (rather than by fiat, arbitrarily and prema-turely; *prior* to the accumulation of knowledge rather than subsequent to it (22) simply for the sake of greater objectivity).

The long-run deficiency characteristics are then the following. It is a basic or instinctoid need if:

1. its absence breeds illness,
2. its presence prevents illness,
3. its restoration cures illness,
4. under certain (very complex) free choice situations, it is preferred by the deprived person over other satisfactions,
5. it is found to be inactive, at a low ebb, or functionally absent in the healthy person.

Two additional characteristics are subjective ones, namely, conscious or unconscious yearning and desire, and feeling of lack or deficiency, as of something missing on the one hand, and, on the other, palatability, ("It tastes good").

One last word on definition. Many of the problems that have plagued the writers in this series as they attempted to define and delimit motivation are a consequence of the exclusive demand for behavioral, externally observable criteria. The original criterion of motivation and the one that is still used by all human beings except behavioral psychologists is the subjective one. I am motivated when I feel desire or want or yearning or wish or lack. No objectively observable state has yet been found that correlates decently with these subjective reports, i.e., no good behavioral definition of motivation has yet been found.

Now of course we ought to keep on seeking for objective correlates of subjective states. On the day when we discover such a public and external indicator of pleasure or of anxiety or of desire, psychology will have jumped forward by a century. But *until* we find it we ought not make believe that we have. Nor ought we neglect the subjective data that we do have. It is unfortunate that we cannot ask a rat to give subjective reports. Fortunately, however, we *can* ask the human being, and I see no reason in the world why we should refrain from doing so until we have a better source of data. If the "objective" psychologists trying to define motivation sometimes seem to be staggering about in the dark, perhaps it is because they have voluntarily blindfolded themselves.

It is these needs which are essentially deficits in the organism, empty holes, so to speak, which must be filled up for health's sake, and furthermore must be filled from without by human beings *other* than the subject that I shall call deficits or deficiency needs for purposes of this exposition and to set them in contrast to another and very different kind of motivation.

There is not a person in this room to whom it would occur to question the statement that we "need" iodine or vitamin C. I remind you that the evidence that we "need" love is of exactly the same type.

In recent years more and more psychologists have found themselves compelled to postulate some tendency to growth or self-perfection to supplement the concepts of equilibrium, homeostasis, tension-reduction, defense and other conserving motivations. This was so for various reasons.

1. *Psychotherapy*. The pressure toward health makes therapy possible. It is an absolute *sine qua non*. If there were no such trend, therapy would be inexplicable to the extent that it goes beyond the building of defenses against pain and anxiety. (Rogers (23), Angyal (2), et cetera).

2. *Brain injured soldiers*. Goldstein's work (13) is well known to all. He found it necessary to invent the concept of self-actualization to explain the reorganization of the person's capacities after injury.

3. *Psychoanalysis*. Some analysts, notably Fromm (12), and Horney (15), have found it impossible to understand even neuroses unless one postulates an impulse toward growth, toward perfection of development, toward the fulfillment of the person's possibilities.

4. *Creativeness*. Much light is being thrown on the general subject of creativeness by the study of healthy growing and grown people, especially when contrasted with sick people. Especially does the theory of art and art education call for a concept of growth and spontaneity (28).

5. *Child Psychology*. Observation of children shows more and more clearly that healthy children *enjoy* growing and moving forward, gaining new skills, capacities and powers. This is in flat contradiction to that version of Freudian theory which conceives of every child as hanging

on desperately to each adjustment that it achieves and to each state of rest or equilibrium. According to this theory, the reluctant and conservative child has continually to be kicked upstairs, out of its comfortable, preferred state of rest *into* a new frightening situation.

While this Freudian conception is continually confirmed by clinicians as largely true for insecure and frightened children, and while it is a little bit true for all human beings, in the main it is *untrue* for healthy, happy, secure children. In these children we see clearly an eagerness to grow up, to mature, to drop the old adjustment as outworn, like an old pair of shoes. We see in them with special clarity not only the eagerness for the new skill but also the most obvious delight in repeatedly enjoying it, the so-called *Funktionslust* of Karl Buhler (8).

For the writers in these various groups, notably Fromm (12), Horney (15), Jung (16), C. Buhler (7), Angyal (2), Rogers (23), and G. Allport (1), and recently some Catholic psychologists (3, 21), growth, individuation, autonomy, self-actualization, self-development, productiveness, self-realization, are all crudely synonymous, designating a vaguely perceived area rather than a sharply defined concept. In my opinion, it is *not* possible to define this area sharply at the present time. Nor is this desirable either, since a definition which does not emerge easily and naturally from well-known facts is apt to be inhibiting and distorting rather than helpful, since it is quite likely to be wrong or mistaken if made by an act of the will on *a priori* grounds. We just don't know enough about growth yet to be able to define it well.

Its meaning can be *indicated* rather than defined, partly by positive pointing, partly by negative contrast, i.e., what it is *not*. For example, it is not equilibrium, homeostasis, tension-reduction, need-reduction, et cetera.

Its necessity has presented itself to its proponents partly because of dissatisfaction (certain newly noticed phenomena simply were not covered by extant theories); partly by positive needs for theories and concepts which would better serve the new humanistic value systems emerging from the breakdown of the older value systems. This paper however derives mostly from a direct study of psychologically healthy individuals. This was under-taken not only for reasons of intrinsic and personal inter-est but also to supply a firmer foundation for the theory of therapy, of pathology and therefore of values. The true goals of education, of family training, of psychotherapy, of self-development, it seems to me, can be discovered only by such a direct attack. The end product of growth teaches us much about the processes of growth. In a recent book (19), I have described what was learned from this study and in addition theorized very freely about various possible consequences for general psychol-ogy of this kind of direct study of good rather than bad human beings, of healthy rather than sick people, of the positive as well as the negative. I must warn you that the data cannot be considered reliable until someone else repeats the study. The possibilities of projection are very real in such a study and of course are unlikely to be detected by the investigator himself. Today I should like to crystallize a little more some of the differences that I have observed to exist between the motivational lives of healthy people and of others, i.e., people motivated by growth needs contrasted with those motivated by the basic needs.

So far as motivational status is concerned, healthy people have sufficiently gratified their basic needs for safety, belongingness, love, respect and self-esteem so that they are motivated primarily by trends to self-actualization (defined as ongoing actualization of poten-tial capacities and talents, as fulfillment of mission or call or fate or vocation, as a fuller knowledge of, and acceptance of, the person's own intrinsic nature, as an unceasing trend toward unity, integration or synergy within the person).

Much to be preferred to this generalized definition would be a descriptive and operational one which I have already published (19). These people are there defined by describing their clinically observed characteristics. These are:

1. Superior perception of reality.
2. Increased acceptance of self, of others and of nature.

3. Increased spontaneity.

4. Increase in problem-centering.

5. Increased detachment and desire for privacy.

6. Increased autonomy, and resistance to enculturation.

7. Greater freshness of appreciation, and richness of emotional reaction.

8. Higher frequency of mystic experiences.

9. Increased identification with the human species.

10. Changed (the clinician would say, improved) interpersonal relations.

11. More democratic character structure.

12. Greatly increased creativeness.

13. Certain changes in the value system.

Furthermore, in this book are described also the limitations imposed upon the definition by unavoidable shortcomings in sampling and in availability of data.

One major difficulty with this conception as so far presented is its somewhat static character.[1] Self-actualization, since I have found it only in older people, tends to be seen as an ultimate or final state of affairs, a far goal, rather than a dynamic process, active throughout life, Being rather than Becoming.

If we define growth as the various processes which bring the person toward ultimate self-actualization, then this conforms better with the observed fact that it is going on *all* the time in the life history. It discourages also the stepwise, *all* or none, saltatory conception of motivational progression toward self-actualization in which the basic needs are completely gratified, one by one, before the next higher one emerges into consciousness. Growth is seen then not only as progressive gratification of basic needs to the point where they disappear, but also in the form of specific growth motivations over and above these basic needs, e.g., talents, capacities, creative tendencies, constitutional potentialities. We are thereby helped also

---

[1] I was made aware of this mostly by Frances Wilson's worth with art education and Gordon Allport's new book on "The Course of Becoming," which I was privileged to read in manuscript. I profited also from discussions with my students in a graduate seminar in motivation theory.

to realize that basic needs and self-actualization do not contradict each other any more than do childhood and maturity. One passes into the other and is a necessary prerequisite for it.

The differentiation between these growth-needs and basic needs which we shall explore in this paper is a consequence of the clinical perception of qualitative differences between the motivational lives of self-actualizers and of other people. These differences, listed below, are fairly well though not perfectly described by the names deficiency-needs and growth-needs. For instance, not all physiological needs are deficits, e.g., sex, elimination, sleep and rest.

At a higher level, needs for safety, belongingness, love and for respect are all clearly deficits. But the need for self-respect is a doubtful case. While the cognitive needs for curiosity-satisfaction and for a system of explanation can easily be considered deficits to be satisfied, as can also the hypothetical need for beauty, the need to create is another matter, as is also the need to express. Apparently not all basic needs are deficits but the needs whose frustration is pathogenic are deficits.

In any case, the psychological life of the person, in very many of its aspects, is lived out differently when he is deficiency-need-gratification-bent and when he is growth-dominated or "metamotivated" or growth-motivated or self-actualizing. The following differences make this clear.

1. Attitude toward impulse: impulse-rejection and impulse-acceptance

Practically all historical and contemporary theories of motivation unite in regarding needs, drives and motivating states in general as annoying, irritating, unpleasant, undesirable, as something to get rid of. Motivated behavior, goal seeking, consummatory responses are all techniques for reducing these discomforts. This attitude is very explicitly assumed in such widely used descriptions of motivation as need reduction, tension reduction, drive reduction, and anxiety reduction.

This approach is understandable in animal psychology and in the behaviorism which is so heavily based upon work with animals. It may be that animals have *only* deficiency needs. Whether or not this turns out to be so, in any case we have treated animals *as if* this were so for the sake of objectivity. A goal object has to be something outside the animal organism so that we can measure the effort put out by the animal in achieving this goal.

It is also understandable that the Freudian psychology should be built upon the same attitude toward motivation that impulses are dangerous and to be fought. After all this whole psychology is based upon experience with sick people, people who in fact suffer from bad experiences with their needs and with their gratifications and frustrations. It is no wonder that such people should fear or even loathe their impulses which have made so much trouble for them and which they handle so badly, and that a usual way of handling them is repression.

This derogation of desire and need has, of course, been a constant theme throughout the history of philosophy, theology and psychology. The Stoics, most hedonists, practically all theologians, many political philosophers and most economic theorists have united in affirming the fact that good or happiness or pleasure is essentially the consequence of amelioration of this unpleasant state of affairs, of wanting, of desiring, of needing.

To put it as succinctly as possible, these people all find desire or impulse to be a nuisance or even a threat and therefore will try generally to get rid of it, to deny it or to avoid it.

This contention is sometimes an accurate report of what is the case. The physiological needs, the needs for safety, for love, for respect, for information are in fact often nuisances for many people, psychic troublemakers, and problem-creators, especially for those who have had unsuccessful experiences at gratifying them and for those who cannot now count on gratification.

Even with these deficiencies, however, the case is very badly overdrawn: one can accept and enjoy one's needs and welcome them to consciousness if (a) past experience with them has been rewarding, and (b) if present and future gratification can be counted on. For example, if one has in general enjoyed food and if good food is now available, the emergence of appetite into consciousness is welcomed instead of dreaded. ("The trouble with eating is that it kills my appetite.") Something like this is true for thirst, for sleepiness, for sex, for dependency needs and for love needs. However, a far more powerful refutation of the "need-is-a-nuisance" theory is found in the recently emerging awareness of, and concern with, growth (self-actualization) motivation.

The multitude of idiosyncratic motives which come under the head of "self-actualization" can hardly be listed since each person has different talents, capacities, potentialities. But some characteristics are general to all of them. And one is that these impulses are desired and welcomed, are enjoyable and pleasant, that the person wants more of them rather than less, and that if they constitute tensions, they are *pleasurable* tensions. The creator welcomes his creative impulses, the talented person enjoys using and expanding his talents.

It is simply inaccurate to speak in such instances of tension-reduction, implying thereby the getting rid of an annoying state. For these states are not annoying.

2. *Differential effects of gratification*

Almost always associated with negative attitudes toward the need is the conception that the primary aim of the organism is to get rid of the annoying need and thereby to achieve a cessation of tension, an equilibrium, a homeostasis, a quiescence, a state of rest, a lack of pain.

The drive or need presses toward its own elimination. Its only striving is toward cessation, toward getting rid of itself, toward a state of not wanting. Pushed to its logical extreme, we wind up with Freud's Death-instinct.

Angyal, Goldstein, G. Allport, C. Buhler and others have effectively criticized this essentially circular position. If the motivational life consists essentially of a defensive removal of irritating tensions, and if the only end product of tension-reduction is a state of passive waiting for more unwelcome irritations to arise and in their turn, to be dispelled, then how does change, or development or movement or direction come about? Why do people improve? Get wiser? What does zest in living mean?

Charlotte Buhler (7) has pointed out that the theory

of homeostasis is different from the theory of rest. The latter theory speaks simply of removing tension which implies that zero tension is best. Homeostasis means coming not to a zero but to an optimum level. This means sometimes reducing tension, sometimes increasing it, e.g., blood pressure may be too low as well as too high.

In either case the lack of constant direction through a lifespan is obvious. In both cases, growth of the personality, increase in wisdom, self-actualization, strengthening of the character, and the planning of one's life are not and cannot be accounted for. Some long-time vector, or directional tendency, must be invoked to make any sense of development through the lifetime (7).

This theory must be put down as an inadequate description even of deficiency motivation. What is lacking here is awareness of the dynamic principle which ties together and interrelates all these separate motivational episodes. The different basic needs are related to each other in a hierarchical order such that gratification of one need and its consequent removal from the center of the stage brings about not a state of rest or Stoic apathy, but rather the emergence into consciousness of another "higher" need; wanting and desiring continues but at a "higher" level. Thus the coming-to-rest theory isn't adequate even for deficiency motivation.

However, when we examine people who are predominantly growth-motivated, the coming-to-rest conception of motivation becomes completely useless. In such people gratification breeds increased rather than decreased motivation, heightened rather than lessened excitement. The appetites become intensified and heightened. They grow upon themselves and instead of wanting less and less, such a person wants more and more of, for instance, education. The person rather than coming to rest becomes more active. The appetite for growth is whetted rather than allayed by gratification. Growth is, *in itself*, a rewarding and exciting process, e.g., the fulfilling of yearnings and ambitions, like that of being a good doctor; the acquisition of admired skills, like playing the violin or being a good carpenter; the steady increase of understanding about people or about the universe, or about oneself; the development of creativeness in whatever field, or, most important, simply the ambition to be a good human being.

Wertheimer (27) long ago stressed another aspect of this same differentiation by claiming, in a seeming paradox, that true goal-seeking activity took up less than 10% of his time. Activity can be enjoyed either intrinsically, for its own sake, or else have worth and value only because it is instrumental in bringing about a desired gratification. In the latter case it loses its value and is no longer pleasurable when it is no longer successful or efficient. More frequently, it is simply *not enjoyed at all*, but only the goal is enjoyed. This is similar to that attitude toward life which values it less for its own sake than because one goes to Heaven at the end of it. The observation upon which this generalization is based is that self-actualizing people enjoy life in general and in practically all its aspects, while most other people enjoy only stray moments of triumph, of achievement or of climax.

Partly this intrinsic validity of living comes from the pleasurableness inherent in growing and in being grown. But it also comes from the ability of healthy people to transform means-activity into end-experience, so that even instrumental activity is enjoyed as if it were end activity (19). Growth motivation may be long-term in character. Most of a lifetime may be involved in becoming a good psychologist or a good artist. All equilibrium or homeostasis or rest theories deal only with short-term episodes, each of which have nothing to do with each other. Allport particularly has stressed this point. Planfulness and looking into the future, he points out, are of the central stuff or healthy human nature. He agrees (1) that "Deficit motives do, in fact, call for the reduction of tension and restoration of equilibrium. Growth motives, on the other hand, maintain tension in the interest of distant and often unattainable goals. As such they distinguish human from animal becoming, and adult from infant becoming."

3. Clinical effects of gratification

Deficit-need gratifications and growth-need gratifications have differential subjective and objective effects upon the personality. If I may phrase what I am groping for here in a very generalized way, it is this: Satisfying deficiencies avoids illness; growth satisfactions produce positive health. I must grant that this will be difficult to pin down for research purposes at this time. And yet there is a real clinical difference between fending off threat or attack and positive triumph and achievement, between protecting, defending and preserving oneself and reaching out for fulfillment, for excitement and for enlargement. I have tried to express this as a contrast between living fully and *preparing* to live fully, between growing up and being grown.

4. Different kinds of pleasure

Erich Fromm (12, p. 186) has made an interesting and important effort to distinguish higher from lower pleasures, as have so many others before him. This is a crucial necessity for breaking through subjective ethical relativity and is a prerequisite for a scientific value theory.

He distinguishes scarcity-pleasure from abundance-pleasure, the "lower" pleasure of satiation of a need from the "higher" pleasure of production, creation and growth of insight. The glut, the relaxation, and the loss of tension that follows deficiency-satiation can at best be called "relief" by contrast with the *Funktionslust*, the ecstasy, the serenity that one experiences when functioning easily, perfectly and at the peak of one's powers—in overdrive, so to speak.

"Relief," depending so strongly on something that disappears, is itself more likely to disappear. It must be less stable, less enduring, less constant than the pleasure accompanying growth, which can go on forever.

5. Attainable and unattainable goal states

Deficiency-need gratification tends to be episodic and climactic. The most frequent schema here begins with an instigating, motivating state which sets off motivated behavior designed to achieve a goal-state, which, mounting gradually and steadily in desire and excitement, finally reaches a peak in a moment of success and consummation. From this peak curve of desire, excitement and pleasure fall rapidly to a plateau of quiet tension-release, and lack of motivation.

This schema, though not universally applicable, in any case contrasts very sharply with the situation in growth-motivation, for here characteristically there is no climax or consummation, no orgasmic moment, no end-state, even no goal if this be defined climactically. Growth is instead a continued, more or less steady upward or forward development. The more one gets, the more one wants so that this kind of wanting is endless and can never be attained or satisfied.

It is for this reason that the usual separation between instigation, goal-seeking behavior, the goal object and the accompanying affect breaks down completely. The behaving is itself the goal, and to differentiate the goal of growth from the instigation to growth is impossible. They too are the same.

6. Species-wide goals and idiosyncratic goals

The deficit-needs are shared by all members of the human species and to some extent by other species as well. Self-actualization is idiosyncratic since every person is different. The deficits, i.e., the species requirements, must ordinarily be fairly well satisfied before real individuality can develop fully.

Just as all trees need sun, water, and foods from the environment, so do all people need safety, love and status from *their* environment. However, in both cases this is just where real development of individuality can begin, for once satiated with these elementary, species-wide necessities, each tree and each person proceeds to develop in his own style, uniquely, using these necessities for his own private purposes. In a very tangible sense, development then becomes more determined from within rather than from without.

7. Dependence and independence of the environment

The needs for safety, belongingness, love relations and for respect can be satisfied only by other people, i.e., only from outside the person. This means considerable dependence on the environment. A person in this dependent position cannot really be said to be governing him-

self, or in control of his own fate. He *must* be beholden
to the sources of supply of needed gratifications. Their
wishes, their whims, their rules and laws govern him and
must be appeased lest he jeopardize his sources of supply.
He *must* be to an extent "other-directed" and *must* be
sensitive to other people's approval, affection and good
will. This is the same as saying that he must adapt and
adjust by being flexible and responsive and by changing
himself to fit the external situation. *He* is the dependent
variable; the environment is the fixed, independent variable.

Because of this, the deficiency-motivated man must be
more afraid of the environment, since there is always the
possibility that it may fail or disappoint him. We now
know that this kind of anxious dependence breeds hostil-
ity as well. All of which adds up to a lack of freedom,
more or less, depending on the good fortune or bad fortune of the individual.

In contrast, the self-actualizing individual, by definition gratified in his basic needs, is far less dependent, far
less beholden, far more autonomous and self-directed.
Far from needing other people, growth-motivated people
may actually be hampered by them. I have already reported their special liking for privacy, for detachment and
for meditativeness.

Such people become far more self-sufficient and self-
contained. The determinants which govern them are
now primarily inner ones, rather than social or environmental. They are the laws of their own inner nature,
their potentialities and capacities, their talents, their
latent resources, their creative impulses, their needs to
know themselves and to become more and more integrated and unified, more and more aware of what they
really are, of what they really want, of what their call or
vocation or fate is to be.

Since they depend less on other people, they are less
ambivalent about them, less anxious and also less hostile,
less needful of their praise and their affection. They are
less anxious for honors, prestige and rewards.

Autonomy or relative independence of environment
means also relative independence of adverse external circumstances, such as ill fortune, hard knocks, tragedy,

stress, deprivation. As Allport has stressed, the notion of the human being as essentially reactive, the S-R man we might call him, who is set into motion by external stimuli, becomes completely ridiculous and untenable for self-actualizing people. The sources of *their* actions are internal rather than external. This relative independence of the outside world and its wishes and pressures, does not mean of course lack of intercourse with it. It means only that in these contacts, the self-actualizer's wishes and plans are the primary determiners, and that the environment becomes more and more a means to his ends. This I have called psychological freedom, contrasting it with geographical freedom.

Allport's very expressive contrast (1) between "opportunistic" and "propriate" determination of behavior parallels very closely our outer-determined, inner-determined opposition. It reminds us also of the uniform agreement among biological theorists in considering increasing autonomy and independence of environmental stimuli as *the* defining characteristics of full individuality, of true freedom, of the whole evolutionary process (29).

8. *Interested and disinterested interpersonal relations*

In essence, the deficit-motivated man is far more dependent upon other people than is the man who is predominantly growth-motivated. He is more "interested," more needful, more attached, more desirous.

This dependency colors and limits interpersonal relations. To see people primarily as need-gratifiers or as sources of supply is an abstractive act. They are seen not as wholes, as complicated, unique individuals, but rather from the point of view of usefulness. What in them is not related to the perceiver's needs is either overlooked altogether, or else bores, irritates, or threatens. This parallels our relations with cows, horses and sheep, as well as with waiters, taxicab drivers, porters, policemen or others whom we *use*.

Fully disinterested, desireless, objective and holistic perception of another human being becomes possible only when nothing is needed from him, only when *he* is not needed. Idiographic, aesthetic perception of the whole person is far more possible for self-actualizing people, and furthermore approval, admiration, and love are based less upon gratitude for usefulness and more upon the objective, intrinsic qualities of the perceived person. He is admired for objectively admirable qualities rather than because he flatters or praises. He is loved because he is love-worthy rather than because he gives out love. This is what will be discussed below as unneeded love.

One characteristic of "interested" and need-gratifying relations to other people is that to a very large extent these need-gratifying persons are interchangeable. Since, for instance, the adolescent girl needs admiration per se, it therefore makes little difference who supplies this admiration; one admiration-supplier is about as good as another. So also for the love-supplier or the safety-supplier.

Disinterested, unrewarded, useless, desireless perception of the other as unique, as independent, as end-in-himself, in other words as a person rather than as a tool is the more difficult, the more hungry the perceiver is for deficit satisfaction. A "high-ceiling" interpersonal psychology, i.e., an understanding of the highest possible development of human relationships, cannot base itself on deficit theory of motivation.

9. Ego-centering and ego-transcendence

We are confronted with a difficult paradox when we attempt to describe the complex attitude toward the self or ego of the growth-oriented, self-actualized person. It is just this person, in whom ego-strength is at its height, who most easily forgets or transcends the ego, who can be most problem-centered, most self-forgetful, most spontaneous in his activities, most homonomous, to use Angyal's term (2). In such people, absorption in perceiving, in doing, in enjoying, in creating can be very complete, very integrated and very pure.

This ability to center upon the world rather than to be self-conscious, egocentric and gratification-oriented becomes the more difficult the more need-deficits the person has. The more growth-motivated the person is the more problem-centered can he be, and the more he can leave self-consciousness behind him as he deals with the objective world.

10. *Interpersonal psychotherapy and intrapersonal psychogogy*

A major characteristic of people who seek psychotherapy is a former and/or present deficiency of basic-need gratification. To a larger extent than the Freudians are yet willing to admit, neurosis is a deficiency-disease. Because this is so, a basic necessity for cure is supplying what has been lacking or making it possible for the patient to do this himself. Since these supplies come from other people, ordinary therapy *must* be interpersonal.

But this fact has been very badly over-generalized. It is true that people whose deficiency needs have been gratified and who are primarily growth-motivated are by no means exempt from conflict, unhappiness, anxiety, and confusion. In such moments they too are apt to seek help and may very well turn to interpersonal therapy. And yet it is unwise to forget that *more* frequently the problems and the conflicts of the growth-motivated person are customarily solved by himself by turning inward in a meditative way, i.e., self-searching rather than seeking for help from someone. Even in principle, many of the tasks of self-actualization are largely intrapersonal, such as the making of plans, the discovery of self, the selection of potentialities to develop, the construction of a life-outlook.

In the theory of personality improvement, a place must be reserved for self-improvement and self-searching contemplation and meditation. In the later stages of growth the person is essentially alone and can rely only upon himself. This improvement of an already well person Oswald Schwarz has called psychogogy. If psychotherapy makes sick people not-sick and removes symptoms, then psychogogy takes up where therapy leaves off and tries to make not-sick people healthy. I was interested to notice in Rogers' recent book (23) that successful therapy raised the patients' average score in The Willoughby Maturity Scale from the twenty-fifth to the fiftieth percentile. Who shall then lift him to the seventy-fifth percentile? Or the one hundredth? And are we not likely to need new principles and techniques to do this with?

11. *Instrumental learning and personality change*

So-called learning theory in this country has based itself almost entirely on deficit-motivation with goal objects usually external to the organism, i.e., learning the best way to satisfy a need. For this reason, among others, our psychology of learning is a very limited body of knowledge, useful only in small areas of life and of real interest only to other "learning theorists."

This is of very little help in solving the problems of growth and self-actualization. Here the techniques of repeatedly acquiring from the outside world satisfactions of motivational deficiencies are much less needed. Associative learning and canalizations give way more to perceptual learning (20), to the increase of insight and understanding, to knowledge of self and to the steady growth of personality, i.e., increased synergy, integration and inner consistency. Change becomes much less an acquisition of habits or associations one by one, and much more a total change of the total person, i.e., a new person rather than the same person with some habits added like new external possessions.

This kind of character-change-learning means changing a very complex, highly integrated, holistic organism, which in turn means that many impacts will make no change at all because more and more such impacts will be rejected as the person becomes more stable and more autonomous.

The most important learning experiences reported to me by my subjects were very frequently single life experiences such as tragedies, deaths, traumata, conversions, sudden insights, which forced change in the life-outlook of the person and consequently in everything that he did. (Of course the so-called "working through" of the tragedy or of the insight took place over a longer period of time but this too was not a matter of associative learning.)

To the extent that growth consists in peeling away inhibition and constraints and then permitting the person to "be himself," to emit behavior—"radioactively," as it were—rather than to repeat it, to allow his inner nature to express itself, to this extent the behavior of self-actualizers is unlearned, created and released rather than acquired, expressive rather than coping. (19, p. 180.)

12. *Deficiency-motivated and growth-motivated perception*

What may turn out to be the most important difference of all is the greater closeness of deficit-satisfied people to the realm of Being (26). Psychologists have never yet been able to claim this vague jurisdiction of the philosophers, this area dimly seen but nevertheless having undoubted basis in reality. But it may now become feasible through the study of self-fulfilling individuals to have our eyes opened to all sorts of basic insights, old to the philosophers but new to us.

For instance, I think that our understanding of perception and therefore of the perceived world will be very much changed and enlarged if we study carefully the distinction between need-interested and need-disinterested or desireless perception. Because the latter is so much more concrete and less abstracted and selective, it is possible for such a person to see more easily the intrinsic nature of the percept. He can perceive simultaneously the opposites, the dichotomies, the polarities, the contradictions and the incompatibles (19, pp. 232-4). It is as if less developed people lived in an Aristotelian world in which classes and concepts have sharp boundaries and are mutually exclusive and incompatible, e.g., male-female, selfish-unselfish, adult-child, angel-devil, kind-cruel, good-bad. A is A and everything else is not A in the Aristotelian logic, and never the twain shall meet. But seen by self-actualizing people is the fact that A and not-A interpenetrate and are one, that any person is simultaneously good *and* bad, male *and* female, adult *and* child. One can not place a whole person on a continuum, only an abstracted aspect of a person.

We may not be aware when *we* perceive in a need-determined way. But we certainly are aware of it when *we* ourselves are perceived in this way, e.g., simply as a money-giver, a food-supplier, a safety-giver, someone to depend on, or as a waiter or other anonymous servant or means-object. When this happens we don't like it at all. We want to be taken for ourselves, as complete and whole individuals. We dislike being perceived as useful objects or as tools. We dislike being "used."

Because self-actualizing people ordinarily do not have to abstract need-gratifying qualities nor see the person as a tool, it is much more possible for them to take a non-valuing, non-judging, non-interfering, non-condemning attitude towards others, a desirelessness, a "choiceless awareness" (17). This permits much clearer and more insightful perception and understanding of what is there. This is the kind of untangled, uninvolved, detached perception that surgeons and therapists are supposed to try for and which self-actualizing people attain *without* trying for.

Especially when the structure of the person or object seen is difficult, subtle and not obvious is this difference in style of perception most important. Especially then must the perceiver have respect for the nature of the object. Perception must then be gentle, delicate, un-intruding, undemanding, able to fit itself passively to the nature of things as water gently soaks into crevices. It must *not* be the need-motivated kind of perception which *shapes* things in a blustering, overriding, exploiting, purposeful fashion, in the manner of a butcher chopping apart a carcass.

The most efficient way to perceive the intrinsic nature of the world is to be more passive than active, determined as much as possible by the intrinsic organization of that which is perceived and as little as possible by the nature of the perceiver. This kind of detached, Taoist, passive, non-interfering awareness of all the simultaneously existing aspects of the concrete, has much in common with some descriptions of the aesthetic experience and of the mystic experience. The stress is the same. Do we see the real, concrete world or do we see our own system of rubrics, motives, expectations and abstractions which we have projected onto the real world? Or, to put it very bluntly, do we see or are we blind?

NEEDED LOVE AND UNNEEDED LOVE

The love need as ordinarily studied, for instance by Bowlby (5), Spitz (24), and Levy (18), is a deficit need.

It is a hole which has to be filled, an emptiness into which love is poured. If this healing necessity is not available, severe pathology results (5, 18); if it *is* available at the right time, in the right quantities and with proper style, then pathology is averted. Intermediate states of pathology and health follow upon intermediate states of thwarting or satiation. If the pathology is not too severe and if it is caught early enough, replacement therapy can cure. That is to say, the sickness, "love-hunger," can be cured in certain cases by making up the pathological deficiency. Love hunger is a deficiency disease exactly as is salt hunger or the avitaminoses.

The healthy person, not having this deficiency, does not need to give or to receive love except in steady, small maintenance doses and he may even do without these for periods of time. But if motivation is entirely a matter of satisfying deficits and thus getting rid of needs, then a crucial paradox results. Satisfaction of the need should cause it to disappear, which is to say that people who have stood in satisfying love relationships are precisely the people who should be *less* likely to give and to receive love! But clinical study of very healthy people, who have been love-need-satiated, shows that they are far *more*—not less—loving people than others.

This finding in itself exposes very clearly the inadequacy of ordinary (deficiency-need-centered) motivation theory and indicates how inescapable is the necessity for "metamotivation theory" (or growth-motivation, or self-actualization theory).

I have already described in a preliminary fashion (19) the contrasting dynamics of B-love (love for the Being of another person, unneeded love, unselfish love) and D-love (deficiency-love, love need, selfish love) and further findings will be set forth in detail in a future publication. At this point, I wish only to use these two contrasting groups of people to exemplify and illustrate some of the generalizations made in this paper.

1. B-Love is welcomed into consciousness, and is completely enjoyed. Since it is non-possessive, and is admiring rather than needing, it makes no trouble and is practically always gratifiable.

2. It can never be sated; it may be enjoyed without

end. It usually grows greater rather than disappearing. It is intrinsically enjoyable. It is end rather than means.

3. The B-love experience is often described as being the same as and having the same effects as the aesthetic experience or the mystic experience.

4. The therapeutic and psychogogic effects of experiencing B-love are very profound and widespread. Similar are the characterological effects of the relatively pure love of a healthy mother for her baby, or the perfect love of their God that some mystics have described. The details are too complex for description here.

5. B-love is, beyond the shadow of a doubt, a richer, "higher," more valuable subjective experience than D-love (which all B-lovers have also previously experienced). This preference is also reported by my other older, more average subjects, many of whom experience both kinds of love simultaneously in varying combinations.

6. D-love *can* be gratified. The concept "gratification" hardly applies at all to admiration-love for another person's admiration-worthiness and love-worthiness.

7. In B-love there is a minimum of anxiety-hostility. For all practical human purposes, it may even be considered to be absent. There *can*, of course, be anxiety-for-the-other. In D-love one must always expect some degree of anxiety-hostility.

8. B-lovers are more independent of each other, more autonomous, less jealous or threatened, less needful, more individual, more disinterested, but also simultaneously more eager to help the other toward self-actualization, more proud of his triumphs, more altruistic, generous and fostering.

9. The truest, most penetrating perception of the other is made possible by B-love. It is as much a cognitive as an emotional-conative reaction, as I have already emphasized (19, pp. 257, 260). So impressive is this, and so often validated by other people's later experience, that, far from accepting the common platitude that love makes people blind, I become more and more inclined to think of the *opposite* as true, namely that non-love makes us blind.

10. Finally I may say that B-love, in a profound but testable sense, creates the partner. It gives him a self-

image, it gives him self-acceptance, a feeling of love-worthiness and respect-worthiness, all of which permit him to grow. It is a real question whether the full development of the human being is possible without it.

REFERENCES

1. ALLPORT, G., *The Course of Becoming*. New Haven: Yale University Press, 1955.
2. ANGYAL, A., *Foundations for a Science of Personality*. New York: Commonwealth Fund, 1941.
3. ARNOLD, M., and GASSON, J., *The Human Person*. New York: Ronald Press, 1954.
4. BANHAM, K. M., The development of affectionate behavior in infancy. *J. gen. Psychol.*, 1950, 76, 283-289.
5. BOWLBY, J., *Maternal Care and Mental Health*. Geneva: World Health Organization, 1952.
6. BUBER, M., *I and Thou*. Edinburgh: T. & T. Clark, 1937.
7. BÜHLER, C., Motivation and personality. *Dialectica*, 1951, 5, 312-361.
8. BÜHLER, K., *Die geistige Entwicklung des Kindes*, 4th ed. Jena: Fischer, 1924.
9. CANNON, W. B., *Wisdom of the Body*. New York: W. W. Norton, 1932.
10. FREUD, S., *An Outline of Psychoanalysis*. New York: W. W. Norton, 1949.
11. FREUD, S., *Beyond the Pleasure Principle*. International Psychoanalytic Press, 1922.
12. FROMM, E., *Man For Himself*. New York: Rinehart, 1947.
13. GOLDSTEIN, K., *Human Nature from the Point of View of Psychopathology*. Cambridge: Harvard University Press, 1940.
14. GOLDSTEIN, K., *The Organism*. New York: American Book Co., 1939.
15. HORNEY, K., *Neurosis and Human Growth*. New York: W. W. Norton, 1950.
16. JUNG, C. G., *Psychological Reflections*. (Jacobi, J., editor), New York: Pantheon Books, 1953.
17. KRISHNAMURTI, J., *The First and Last Freedom*. New York: Harper, 1954.
18. LEVY, D., *Maternal Overprotection*. New York: Columbia University Press, 1943.
19. MASLOW, A. H., *Motivation and Personality*. New York: Harper, 1954.
20. MURPHY, G., and HOCHBERG, J., Perceptual development: some tentative hypotheses, *Psychol. Rev.*, 1951, 58, 332-349.

21. NUTTIN, J., *Psychoanalysis and Personality*. New York: Sheed and Ward, 1953.

22. RITCHIE, B. F., Comments on Professor Farber's paper. In Marshall R. Jones (Ed.), *Nebraska Symposium on Motivation*, 1954, 46-50.

23. ROGERS, C., *Psychotherapy and Personality Change*. Chicago: University of Chicago Press, 1954.

24. SPITZ, R., Anaclitic depression. *Psychoanal. Study of the Child*. 1946, 2, 313-342.

25. SUTTIE, I., *Origins of Love and Hate*. London: Kegan Paul, 1935.

26. TILLICH, P., *The Courage To Be*. New Haven: Yale University Press, 1952.

27. WERTHEIMER, M., Unpublished lectures at the New School for Social Research, 1935-6.

28. WILSON, F., Unpublished papers on art education and psychology, 1954.

29. WOODGER, J., *Biological Principles*. New York: Harcourt, Brace, 1929.

7

Motivations Leading to Social Behavior

LEON FESTINGER
University of Minnesota

In the course of a symposium where six persons talk about motivation, each focusing on a different problem area within psychology, one may perhaps acquire the impression that different kinds of motivation instigate behavior in these various areas. A person interested in the area of learning does not, usually, talk about the same human motives as a person who concerns himself with personality. And a person who deals with social behavior will generally find still other motivations to talk about. I suspect this indicates nothing more than that a person who is concerned with a specific problem area likes to think in terms which are most easily applicable to the data he finds. I am, however, skeptical that there are human motivations which lead solely, or even primarily, to social behavior. In other words, I think that the same motivations which explain non-social behavior will also have their uses in explaining some social behavior.

Before I create any misunderstanding, however, I want to say quickly that this does not mean that social psychologists should confine themselves to talking about the same kinds of motivations that other psychologists talk about. To do that would imply that psychologists already knew all about, and had correctly conceptualized, human motivation. What I do mean to imply by the preceding discussion is that any motivation conceptualized within a theoretical scheme to account for social behavior

Reprinted from *The Nebraska Symposium* edited by Marshall R. Jones, University of Nebraska Press, 1954, with permission of the author and publishers.

should, at a minimum, have some implications for non-social behavior. It would also be very nice to have it operate in the other direction too.

In other words, in thinking of motivation in connection with social behavior, it seems to me we want to ask the following kind of question: Under what conditions does some particular human motive lead to social behavior?

In some instances this question will lead the social psychologist away from a concern with the motivation itself. For example, it is easy to see that in some instances a condition of hunger will lead to social behavior. One kind of situation in which this would happen occurs when some other person or persons control whether or not the individual can get food. Thus, a child might want to eat at a time when his parents ordinarily prohibit eating. Getting food would then require social action. But once we have stated this aspect of the situation it becomes clear that the nature of the motivation is not the important thing for the social psychologist to think about. The important thing to study would be situations where other persons have power in the sense that they control the gratifications or satisfactions which the individual seeks. And so the social psychologist would properly be led in his investigation to emphasize this kind of relationship rather than the motivations which may operate.

There are, however, other motivations, which because of the nature of the world in which people live, characteristically lead to social behavior. In these cases the social psychologist must concern himself with the motivation itself as much as with the characteristics of the situation. We will, in the remainder of this paper, conceptualize one such motive which itself is quite non-social in character and develop the way in which social behavior derives from it. Since the motivation we will discuss is non-social in character, it clearly will sometimes lead to behavior which is not within the realm of social psychology. We will not, however, dwell on this aspect of it. It seems to me sufficient, at the present, to develop those aspects which do lead to social behavior as long as it is clear that there are also non-social implications.

Let us start by looking at some rather molar aspects of

human behavior. It would seem, at least from casual observation, that the human organism expends considerable energy just finding out about the world in which he lives. He explores, he tries things out, or is just curious about things. This kind of behavior is, of course, especially noticeable in children but is equally marked in adults who find themselves in a new situation. It would almost seem as though there is a positive motivation to know one's environment.

Persons also try to find out what they can and cannot do in the environment in which they live. This represents a kind of exploration of themselves which is essentially similar to the exploration of the environment. Taken together we can say that the human being attempts to know what exists in the world around him and to know what his possibilities of action are in that world.

But let us examine somewhat more closely the nature of this motivation. It is not sufficient for the individual just to have *some* idea of the world around him. He must also feel that what he knows is correct knowledge. If he becomes convinced that some idea of his is incorrect, he is likely to discard it and accept some other idea which he now feels is correct. Similarly, it is not enough for the individual to have vague and inexact ideas concerning his possibilities for action in his environment. It seems to be important for persons to know quite precisely what their abilities are, what they can and cannot do.

Let us attempt to state this a bit more formally. We will assume that there is a motivation in the human organism to hold *correct* opinions, beliefs and ideas about the world in which he lives and to know *precisely* what his abilities enable him to do in this world.

So far we have said nothing about social behavior in relation to this motivation. We are led to a consideration of social processes, however, when we begin to ask the next set of questions about behavior resulting from this motivation. How do persons go about assuring themselves that their opinions and beliefs are correct and how do they go about obtaining precise evaluations of their abilities?

There are some instances in which this is a straightforward process which might be called "reality testing" in the environment. A person who thinks the temperature outdoors is below the freezing point can look at a thermometer and check this opinion. Or if he doesn't trust thermometers, and he has patience, he can put a dish of water outdoors and wait to see if it freezes. To examine a comparable case concerning abilities, let us imagine a person who has no use for an air-rifle except to shoot squirrels. If he wants to know whether or not his ability is good enough to accomplish the single purpose, namely, can he shoot squirrels with an air-rifle, it is possible for him, city ordinances permitting, to try to do it and find out whether indeed he can.

There are some other instances where a "reality test" in the environment is possible but may be difficult to carry out. If a person thinks a certain species of mushroom is poisonous he will not be eager to test this by eating them. A person who wonders whether or not he can jump across a stream, might likewise be hesitant to test this directly.

There are still other instances where a "reality test" is impossible or simply does not serve any purpose at all. A person who believes, say, that reincarnations occur, or that a war is inevitable, has no way at all to test the correctness of these beliefs in the environment. There is no "reality test" available at all for opinions and beliefs such as these. Or let us imagine a high school student who wants to know whether his intellectual ability is such as to enable him to go through college. He also cannot adequately evaluate this ability in the real world. Clearly, going to college and seeing what happens would give him an evaluation of his ability for that purpose, but it is not possible to "reality test" his ability before going to college. In the case of abilities it is particularly true that, even when a clear and unambiguous "performance score" is available, it may not provide a satisfactory evaluation because of the large variety of situations for which the ability is relevant and the large number of purposes which make the ability important. Also important is the frequent desire to evaluate the ability *before* engaging in the action which would test it.

What, then, does the individual do in instances where his opinions or his abilities cannot be evaluated directly by testing against the environment? Under these circumstances the person "tests himself" against, or more specifically, compares himself with, other persons. In this way the non-social motivation which we have elaborated leads to social behavior. For the rest of this paper we will develop some ideas about this social comparison process and discuss some results of experiments relating to it.

Let us examine the nature of this social comparison process and how it enables the individual to evaluate his opinions and abilities in the absence of the possibility of so-called "reality tests." To the extent that he cannot test an opinion in the "real world" he compares his opinion with the opinions held by others with whom he associates. If these others hold the same opinion which he does, then he feels his own opinion is correct. If these others with whom he compares hold different opinions, then he tends to feel that his own opinion is perhaps incorrect. Agreement with others, then, provides him with the same subjective feeling of correctness that would result from a "reality test" which supported his opinion.

Similarly, in the case of evaluation of abilities, the person will compare his own performance with the performance of others to the extent that it is difficult to find out precisely what he can or cannot do by testing against the real world. Then, if the others with whom he compares his performance are relatively close to him he feels subjectively that he knows the level of his ability. If the others are far away from him in their performance then he still does not know precisely just how good his ability is. Let us take as an illustration a person who tries to find out precisely how intelligent he is. Let us remember that his motivation is to know what his ability does and does not permit him to do in the real world in which he lives and acts. Simply knowing his score on some intelligence test does not tell him this. It does, however, allow him to compare himself with others. Suppose the others with whom he compares himself are all very divergent from himself in their score. He then knows that his possibilities for action in the world are very different from theirs. But this is negative knowledge and he still does not know precisely what he himself can do. Consider, however, the case where the others with whom he compares himself have scores very close to his own. He then knows that his own possibilities for action in the environment are identical or very similar to those for these other persons. This gives him the subjective feeling of knowing what he can or cannot do in the same way that having others agree with one's opinion gives the person a subjective feeling that his own opinion is correct.

In the evaluation of both abilities and opinions, then, the motivation we have assumed leads to pressures toward uniformity. That is, we would predict tendencies to draw closer together with others on both opinions and abilities. We would also, accordingly, expect to see behavior which moves persons closer together when a large discrepancy among them exists initially.

Let us examine some experimental data to see if such movement toward uniformity does indeed occur both for opinions and for abilities. Let us first consider opinions. I will describe an experiment by Festinger and Thibaut (6) which provides an illustration of this movement towards uniformity. In this experiment groups were given a problem to discuss which was chosen so as to produce initially wide divergence of opinion in the group. In half of the groups a problem was used concerning which there would be little resistance to changing opinions. It was a problem concerning strategy in a football game. In the other groups a problem was chosen such that there would be strong resistance against changing opinions on it. This was a problem concerning what to do with a delinquent boy. In addition, three different sets of instructions were used to experimentally vary the strength of the pressure towards uniformity in the group. Figure 1 shows the data from this experiment.

In the condition labeled "high pressure toward uniformity" the groups were told they were supposed to come to agreement. This condition, of course, does not interest us too much because the pressure towards uniformity was imposed by the experimenter. It does, however, serve as an extreme to compare with the other conditions where the experimenter did not impose the pressure.

In the condition labeled "Medium Pressure" they were

told there was a correct answer and the group would be scored according to how many arrived at this correct answer. It is clear that in this condition there would be pressure toward uniformity only to the extent that agreeing with others made them feel their opinion was correct. The experimental instructions made it important to be correct.

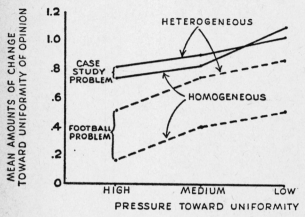

Fig. 1. *Mean amounts of change toward uniformity of opinion*

In the condition labeled "Low Pressure" they were simply asked to discuss the problem. Here the pressure towards uniformity would be less than in the "medium" condition because the importance of being correct in one's opinion was less.

The measure of movement towards uniformity was calculated by dividing the standard deviation of the opinions in each group at the end of the discussion by the standard deviation at the beginning of the discussion. Thus an index lower than 1.0 would indicate change towards uniformity in the group. For the moment let us ignore the differences between the conditions labeled Heterogeneous and Homogeneous in the figure. We shall return to this later on.

It is clear from inspection of the figure that in all

cases greater movement towards uniformity results from greater pressure in that direction. It is also clear that for the case study problem where opinions were more resistant to change, the observed movement towards uniformity is less. In the "low pressure" condition for this problem there is no movement towards uniformity at all. For the football problem, where the resistance to changing opinions is weaker, there is appreciable movement towards uniformity even under "low pressure." Although we cannot take the time here to discuss all the experiments which have been done on this problem, we may say that this movement towards uniformity is also clearly shown in experiments by Back (1), by Gerard (9) and others. We may safely conclude that, at least with respect to opinions, this is a demonstrated phenomenon.

Before we turn to an examination of an experiment to see whether the same thing holds true for abilities, however, we must discuss briefly some differences which we may expect to exist between opinions and abilities in movement toward uniformity. We already have seen that the existence of pressures toward uniformity does not guarantee that actual movement toward uniformity will occur. The resistance to change of opinion may be sufficiently strong so that, in spite of considerable attempts to influence others, no actual movement towards uniformity is observed. This resistance to change would, of course, be quite strong when dealing with abilities since it is frequently difficult if not impossible to change them and even where they can be changed it would take considerable time to complete the change. In dealing with it experimentally we must, then, attempt to set up a situation which will reveal the tendency even though the actual change may not be accomplished.

The experiment which I shall describe is being conducted by Brehm and myself. In this experiment a group situation is created so that: (1) the performance of each member relevant to an important ability is revealed, and (2) there is produced a wide spread of performance under circumstances where it is possible to measure evidences of attempted movement toward uniformity.

This was done in the following way: prospective subjects were told that we were conducting experiments on the most effective methods of training persons in how to make accurate judgments about other people. The importance of this ability was stressed. Those who were interested in such training were given an opportunity to volunteer.

Five subjects were scheduled together for each experimental session. The training procedure, they were told, consisted of getting to know each other and then making judgments about what each of the others would do in a number of hypothetical situations. After each hypothetical situation was described each member wrote a few sentences stating what he thought each other person in the group would do in that situation. They were free to write anything they chose to. After they had made their judgments about what each other person would do, each one scored the four judgments which had been made about himself for accuracy. In this way, they were told, we would have a good measure, for each person, of how well he could make such judgments about other people. This not only served as a means of getting the subjects to attach importance to the scores they received, but also served an important measurement function. By having each person score the judgments others had made about him, he was given some control over how high they scored on the ability. The scores given to each person would then reveal pressures toward uniformity if such pressures exist.

After each set of judgments they discussed it among themselves and then the experimenter put on the board the scores each of them had received. Actually the scores that were put on the board were predesignated so that, for each of the three hypothetical situations, one person scored consistently very much higher than all the others, another scored consistently very much lower than all the others while the other three subjects scored very close to each other in the middle. Attempted movement toward uniformity would then be revealed in the scores each of them gave to those who were above or below them in reported total. In other words, since the performance score of each person was partially under the control of each other person in the group, attempts to bring others down to, or to bring others up to, one's own score would be indicative of attempts to draw the group closer together in performance.

This experiment is still in progress but in Figure 2 I have summarized some of the data collected thus far. These data are based on 10 groups in each of two conditions. The figure shows the average rating given to the

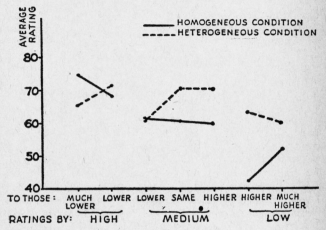

Fig. 2. *Average ratings given on last situation*

judgments made by those who had been scoring above or below the person making the rating. Let us look first at the data for the condition labeled "homogeneous." This is a condition where the subjects felt that the others in the group were the same kinds of people as themselves. We will discuss this factor in detail later. The two points at the left are the average ratings *given* by the subject who was scoring far above the others. The two points on the right are average ratings *given* by the subject scoring far below the others. The three points in the middle are the average ratings by those subjects who were scoring midway between the high and low. The abscissa indicates the score of the person being rated relative to the rater.

It is very clear that in the homogeneous condition the person scoring above the others rates others high. In other

words, he attempts to bring them up to himself. It is
equally clear that the person scoring below the others
rates these others low. He attempts to bring these others
down nearer his own score. In short, in this condition
pressures toward uniformity are operating.

We will return in a moment to a discussion of the
data for the heterogeneous condition.

Thus far we have spoken only about pressure towards
uniformity arising from social comparison without having
said anything about what determines with whom one
compares oneself. People do not compare their opinions
and their abilities with others indiscriminately. They tend
to compare themselves only with those whom they feel
are like them in some way: the same kinds of people, or
ones who have things in common with themselves. We
should then expect different behavior in the presence of
others who are accepted as a relevant comparison group
than in the presence of others who less easily fill this role.

In order to discuss the specifics of these differences in
behavior, however, it is necessary first to examine some of
the various kinds of behavior which would result from
the existence of pressure toward uniformity. In a situation where a wide discrepancy of opinion or ability
exists pressure towards uniformity would manifest itself
in any or all of at least three different ways.

1. There would be evidence of attempts to change
one's own position on the opinion or on the ability. If we
were concerned with opinions we would expect to find
instances of persons changing their mind about the issue
or becoming less confident that their opinion is correct.
If we were concerned with abilities we would expect persons to practice more or to stop practicing depending
upon whether they were above or below most others in
the group. Parenthetically I would like to call attention
at this point to the asymmetry which exists concerning
abilities, namely, differences in behavior depending upon
the direction of the divergence from the group.

2. There would be evidence of attempts to change the
position of others in the group. Considering opinions we
would expect to observe attempts to influence others in
the group so as to cause them to change their opinions
in a direction which would bring them closer to the opin-

ion of the person exerting the influence. In the case of abilities we would expect to see such behavior as hindering others or helping and encouraging others, once more depending upon whether the person is below or above the rest of the group.

3. There would also be evidence of a cessation of comparison with those who were most divergent from one's own opinion or ability. In other words, excluding from one's comparison group those who are too divergent also results in increased uniformity among those with whom one still compares. In the case of opinions we would then expect to find a progressive decrease in communication to those who are most divergent in the group coupled with a tendency to exclude those most divergent persons from the group. In dealing with abilities we would expect to find an acceptance of the different status (either clearly higher or clearly lower as the case might be) for those who were extremely divergent and a cessation of attempts to bring oneself closer together with those persons. Experiments by Back (1), Schachter (11), Festinger, et al. (7), Dreyer (2), and others have demonstrated the existence of all these manifestations of pressure toward uniformity.

Let us now return to consider the factor of homogeneity-heterogeneity, that is, the perception of whether or not others in the group are the same kinds of persons as oneself. We may ask whether the factor of heterogeneity-homogeneity is most likely to affect the tendency to change others, the tendency to change oneself or the tendency to cease comparison with those who are most divergent from one's own position. Since heterogeneity would directly affect the tendency to compare oneself with these other people we might plausibly expect to observe the cessation of comparison as a dominant effect. In other words, if the subject has the perception that the others in the group are different kinds of persons from himself he will be more inclined to stop comparing himself with those in the group who are most divergent.

Let us return to first figure. The curves labeled Heterogeneous are for conditions where the subjects were told that the group was composed of very different kinds of people with different degrees of interest in the problem.

In short, there was an attempt to create a perception of heterogeneity. In the conditions labeled Homogeneous there was an attempt to create a perception of homogeneity by telling them they were selected to be as nearly alike in background and interest in the problem as possible. In accordance with our immediately preceding discussion we would then expect that in the heterogeneous condition there should be a relative cessation of comparison with and communication to those who are most divergent from themselves. This would also result in less movement toward uniformity in the heterogeneous condition than in the homogeneous condition.

We find that groups in the heterogeneous conditions do show much less movement toward uniformity on the football problem than do the groups in the homogeneous condition. For the case study problem, where the resistance to change is high, this difference all but disappears. In this experiment data also were collected concerning the direction of communication, that is, whom the persons attempted to influence. As we would expect, in the heterogeneous condition, for both problems, there is a tendency to stop communicating to the most divergent members of the group. In other words, in the heterogeneous condition there was a tendency to stop comparing themselves with those whose opinions were most different from their own. When the resistance to change of opinion was sufficiently weak to allow change to occur, there was also less movement toward uniformity in the heterogeneous than in the homogeneous conditions.

Now let us look once more at the second figure to see if the same type of effect shows itself with respect to abilities. In this experiment the conditions of homogeneity and heterogeneity were experimentally created by instructions similar to those in the previously mentioned experiment.

It is clear that the same effect does occur. While in the homogeneous condition the ratings they give to others are clearly related to their own scores, this is not at all true of the heterogeneous condition. The average rating given to others is virtually the same for those who are themselves scoring high, medium and low. In short, in the heterogeneous condition there is no longer any evidence of attempted movement toward uniformity within the group. On the contrary, there begins to be evidence of accepting and acknowledging inferior and superior status in others. Thus, those who are scoring high now give significantly lower ratings to those scoring low than to those scoring in the middle. In other words, the high scorers stop trying to bring the very low scorers up to them. Those scoring in the middle also show evidence of cessation of comparison with those who are very different from themselves. They rate the low scorer lower than the others. In other words, accompanying the cessation of comparison is a diminution of attempts to bring that person and oneself closer together. This operates for both opinions and abilities.

An experiment by Hoffman, Festinger and Lawrence (10) shows this effect even more clearly. I would like to describe this experiment in detail since it also leads to the next point which I want to elaborate concerning these pressures toward uniformity.

In this experiment a situation was created where, in a group of three persons, any two could control how well the other person did. This was accomplished in the following manner. In the guise of an intelligence test, each of the three persons in the group was given an identical set of seven assorted triangles. They were told that this part of the test involved making squares out of these triangles. It was possible to make a square out of some of one's own pieces and it was also possible to make a square by sharing pieces with others. There were to be five trials and on each trial the person who succeeded in making the largest square would get 8 points. If on the *first* trial anyone succeeded in making the individual square he would automatically win that trial and get a 12 point bonus, in addition to the 8 points. This individual square, that is, the square that could be made without sharing pieces with others, was extremely difficult to make and since each trial lasted only 4 minutes it was, for all practical purposes, impossible. Just before the end of the first trial, one of the three persons, a paid participant, put his individual square together. He thus received 20 points while each of the others had no points at all as yet.

The only other square that could be made was a large one that simply involved joining together two right angle isosceles triangles. Each of the three persons had one such triangle so that from the second trial through the fifth trial the only question at issue was which two persons would agree to share their pieces to make the square. They were told that the 8 points could be split in any way they agreed on between the two who shared pieces. Thus the four minutes of each trial was spent in bargaining among them as to how they would split the 8 points if they agreed to put their triangles together. During the last four trials, the paid participant behaved so as to try to maximize the number of points he would get by always trying to break up an impending agreement between the other two by offering one or the other more points if he joined with him in making the square. It is clear that the two subjects have complete control over how many points the paid participant gets in these trials. They could cut him out completely or enable him to make many points. Thus, the average number of points which the paid participant does get in these last four trials is a measure of the extent to which the subjects are holding him back and trying to bring themselves and him closer together. This experiment was conducted under conditions where the subjects were given the impression that they were homogeneous or heterogeneous and also under conditions where the test they were taking was seen as very important or relatively unimportant. The homogeneity-heterogeneity variation was accomplished in a manner similar to the other experiments we have already discussed. Variation in importance of the test was accomplished in the following manner. In the high importance condition the subjects were told that this was a new type of intelligence test which had proven to be so superior to any other test that we were now engaged in collecting as much data as possible concerning it. In the low importance condition they were told that this test had been proposed as an intelligence test by some psychologist who had made extravagant claims for its validity. The accumulation of evidence, however, was beginning to show that it was completely worthless. We were doing this study to show once and for all that the test was not any good.

Figure 3 shows the data from this experiment for the high importance and low importance conditions and for the conditions where the subjects were given the impression that the group was homogeneous or that one member of the group was very different from themselves. It is clear that in the heterogeneous condition there is much less evidence of pressure toward uniformity than in the homogeneous condition. For both degress of importance the subjects allow the paid participant to get many more points in the heterogeneous conditions. In fact, in the heterogeneous condition where the test is of little importance to the subjects, the paid participant gets more points than one would expect by chance, thus increasing the discrepancy among them rather than reducing it.

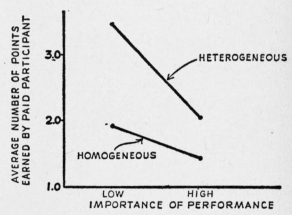

Fig. 3. *Average number of points earned by paid participant in last four trials*

Looking at the figure it is also clear that the importance of the performance also has an appreciable effect on the strength of the pressure towards uniformity. How can we account for this in terms of the motivation we have assumed exists which leads to these pressures toward uniformity? In order to answer this question let us recall briefly the way in which this motivation leads to pressures toward uniformity.

We assumed, we will recall, that persons are motivated to evaluate their opinions and abilities, that is, to know that one's opinions are correct and to know precisely what one is and is not capable of doing. When this cannot be accomplished by reference to the physical world around one, it is accomplished by comparison with other persons. But it can be accomplished only by comparison with others whose opinions or abilities are close to one's own. Anything, then, which affects the strength of the motivation will affect the intensity of the comparison process and consequently will affect the strength of the pressure toward uniformity. Likewise, anything which affects the importance of a particular group as a comparison group will affect the strength of the pressure towards uniformity in that group. The motivation to know precisely what one can or cannot do with respect to an important ability is stronger than it is with respect to an unimportant ability. Consequently, the greater the importance of the ability, the greater is the pressure towards uniformity concerning it. Thus we see, in Figure 3, that where the performance is an important reflection of intelligence the pressure toward uniformity is considerably stronger than where the performance is not important.

The same considerations we have stated above also lead to other derivations. We would expect that the more relevant an opinion or ability is to the functioning of a particular group, the greater would be the pressure toward uniformity in that group concerning that particular opinion or ability. We would expect also that the more attractive a group was to its members, the stronger would be the pressures toward uniformity in that group about issues relevant to the group. This should be true since stronger attraction to a group would make it more important as a comparison group.

Studies dealing with opinion discrepancies in groups have produced data confirming these derivations. An experiment by Gerard (9) showed that the greater the relevance of an issue to immediate action the greater was the pressure toward uniformity in the group as shown by efforts to influence others and by actual movement toward uniformity. Schachter (11) showed that the greater the relevance of an issue to the functioning of the group, the stronger was the degree of rejection of deviates.

The relation between attraction to the group and pressure toward uniformity has also been documented experimentally. Experiments by Back (1) and by Festinger, Gerard, *et al.* (7) have shown that the stronger the attraction to the group the greater are the efforts to change the opinions of others and also the greater are the tendencies to change one's own opinion in the direction of the others. In the previously mentioned experiment by Schachter (11) it was also shown that the greater the attraction to the group the greater was the tendency to reject those who disagreed markedly with the modal opinion in the group.

Because of the limitations of time it is impossible to go into all of these studies on the relation between attraction to the group and pressure toward uniformity in detail. I will, however, describe more thoroughly an experiment recently completed by Festinger, Torrey and Willerman (8) which was designed to test the derivation concerning the relation between attraction to the group and pressure toward uniformity in the case of ability evaluation. I choose to describe this study in detail rather than any of the others because it is so recent that most of you will not already be familiar with it, and also because of the paucity of experiments testing these hypotheses with reference to abilities compared to the relatively large number which have tested them with opinions.

In the previous two experiments dealing with abilities which we have described, in each case the situation was constructed so as to allow the members of the group to have control over how well others scored. In this way it was possible to observe evidence of pressure toward and movement towards uniformity. In the experiment which I will now describe, however, it was decided not to have this kind of condition but rather to establish a more usual type of performance situation in which the scores a person got were completely *out* of the control of the others in the group. We felt it was desirable to do this since it is possible that some of the effects may have been due to the fact that the subjects did perceive that others could control how well they scored.

The following situation was consequently devised. Four subjects were scheduled to appear at the same time. They were told that a new set of tests had recently been made available which had proved very effective over years of research in predicting success in later life. The tests, they were told, actually tested a new ability which had been discovered to be the major factor determining success or failure in later life. This ability was described to them as the ability to make accurate judgments from incomplete information. It was described to them in a manner which made it plausible for this ability to be so important.

There was thus created a situation where, in taking these tests, they were performing with reference to an ability that was important but concerning which they had no previous basis for evaluating their own level of performance. This was done so that the manifestations of pressure toward uniformity in these groups would be as strong as we could possibly make them. If we had dealt instead with a familiar ability, one on which the subjects had pretty good ideas from other comparisons as to how good they were, this would have served to minimize the importance of the group of four people in the laboratory as a reference for comparison.

The subjects were then given three tests. The first test required them to insert, as best they could from guessing, alternate lines which had been deleted from a prose passage. While the experimenter's assistant was scoring these for accuracy they took the second test which involved making judgments about the characteristics of persons from short snatches of written dialogue. These were also scored for accuracy by the experimenter's assistant. The last test involved successive guesses as to which of five lights would light up. This test the subjects scored themselves by recording correct and incorrect predictions. The scores they received, however, were under the control of the experimenter who secretly determined which light would appear after having seen the predictions the subjects made. This last test was arranged in this way to dispel any suspicion any of the subjects may have had.

After each test had been scored the scores they received were written on the blackboard by the experimenter.

Actually, all the scores were predetermined by the experimenter. One member of the group, selected at random, consistently received scores which were a bit lower than the scores received by the other three subjects. These latter three subjects always scored very close together. We thus created a situation where there was a mild discrepancy in performance in a group. We should, consequently, expect to be able to observe some manifestation of pressures toward uniformity among the members. But this raises an interesting problem. Exactly what manifestations of this pressure could we possibly observe in the situation as we had established it?

It is not possible, in this situation, to observe any actual movement toward uniformity the way we could if the scores were under the control of the other members of the group. Nor is the duration of the experiment long enough to be able to observe attempts to practice or to help others and the like. We must then depend for our measurement on determining the actual evaluation that the subjects make of their ability, which, incidentally, would also help to show once more that the pressures toward uniformity, and the social processes involved, stem directly from the motivation to make such an evaluation.

Let us, then, consider what kind of measure would reveal the evaluation people would make of their abilities in the experiment we have described. In dealing with abilities we do not expect the same evaluation irrespective of the direction of deviation from the others in the group. This, of course, is because of the asymmetry which we have mentioned earlier. There is, in the case of abilities, a push upwards; a desire to do better and better which is independent of the pressure toward uniformity. We would then expect deviation from others in the group to result in an evaluation of good or bad performance, depending upon the direction of the deviation. We would also expect to find lack of clarity concerning precisely how good or bad one is if the amount of deviation is very large. Since, in the experiment we are now discussing, we were careful to keep the amount of difference in scores rather small we can ignore this last mentioned factor.

In accordance with this reasoning, after having taken the tests, the subjects were asked to rate on a seven point scale how well they felt they had done. To be consistent with our theory we would expect that among those whose initial attraction to the group was high, the ones who scored below others would feel that they had done very poorly while the ones who had scored equal to or above the others would feel that they had done quite well. Among those who were less attracted to the group at the start, this difference should be considerably smaller.

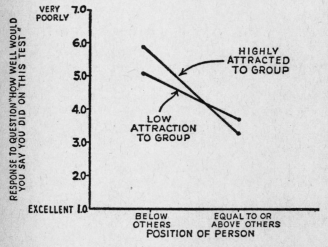

Fig. 4. Average ratings of how well they felt they had done on the test

Figure 4 presents the data from the experiment. It is clear that the results are directly in line with our expectations. Those who score below the others feel that their performance is worse the more they are initially attracted to the group. Those who score equal to or above the others feel their performance is better the more they are

attracted to the group. In other words, the stronger the
attraction to the group, the stronger is the pressure toward uniformity stemming from the need to evaluate the
ability in this group, and, consequently, the greater is
the effect upon their evaluations of the differences which
exist among them.

Since it is integral to the theory we are discussing to
demonstrate the parallel between opinion evaluation and
ability evaluation, I would like to now consider the direct
effect on evaluation of *opinions* of variation in the pressure toward uniformity. In dealing with opinions we
would expect agreement with others to make one more
confident of one's opinion, while disagreement with
others would be expected to reduce one's confidence. The
previously mentioned experiment by Festinger, Gerard
and others (7) shows this to be clearly the case. In this
experiment the distribution of opinion was controlled
by asking each person preliminary to a discussion, to
write down his present opinion on the issue in question.
These were collected and presumably tallied by the
experimenter who then handed back to each person a
fictitious census which showed him to be either in agreement with most of the others or in marked disagreement
with most of the others. They were then asked to state
their confidence in their opinion. Those who had the
impression that most of the others in the group agreed
with them show markedly higher confidence in their
opinions than do those who thought that most of the
other members of the group disagreed with them. In other
words, their evaluation of their opinion did depend upon
this comparison with others.

We would also expect, in line with our hypothesis concerning the relation between pressure toward uniformity
and attraction to the group that among those who felt
that the others disagreed with them, the stronger their
attraction to the group, the less confident should they
become. That is, the more important the group was as a
comparison group for them, the greater should be the
effect on their confidence of finding these others in
disagreement with them. This was indeed found to be
the case although the difference was small and not statis-
tically significant. My own hunch is that, in the experi-

ment, the rating scale on which we asked them to rate their confidence was too unreliable to show the rather small differences that were experimentally created.

Before I conclude I would like to summarize briefly the points I have tried to make. We started out by assuming the existence of a motivation to know that one's opinions are correct and to know precisely what one is and is not capable of doing. From this motivation, which is certainly non-social in character, we have made the following derivations about the conditions under which a social comparison process arises and about the nature of this social comparison process.

1. This social process arises when the evaluation of opinions or abilities is not feasible by testing directly in the environment.
2. Under such circumstances persons evaluate their opinions and abilities by comparison with others.
3. This comparison leads to pressures toward uniformity.
4. There is a tendency to stop comparing oneself with others who are very divergent. This tendency increases if others are perceived as different from oneself in relevant dimensions.
5. Factors such as importance, relevance and attraction to a group which affect the strength of the original motivation will affect the strength of the pressure towards uniformity.

It appears from the experiments I have described here, and from others which I have not had time to go into in detail but which are reported elsewhere (3, 4, 5), that these hypotheses about social comparison processes which I have stated hold equally for opinions and for abilities. This is, of course, not surprising if these social comparison processes for both instances do indeed stem from the same basic motivation.

But this motivation was not observed. It was hypothesized or assumed as is indeed the case with all motivations in spite of the occasional attempts on the part of some psychologists to define a motivation as a pattern of behavior. Dealing with a motivation always amounts to dealing with a construct. Finding, as we have, that the social comparison processes operate the way we expected them to and that they operate in the same way for both opinions and abilities, gives us some confirmation of the theory concerning the motivation to evaluate one's opinions and abilities.

REFERENCES

1. BACK, K., The exertion of influence through social communication, *J. abnorm. soc. Psychol.*, 1951, 46, 9-24.

2. DREYER, A., Behavior in a level of aspiration situation as affected by group comparison, Ph.D. Thesis, 1953, University of Minnesota.

3. FESTINGER, L., Informal social communication, *Psychol. Rev.*, 1950, 57, 271-282.

4. FESTINGER, L., A theory of social comparison processes, *Human Relations*, 1954.

5. FESTINGER, L., SCHACHTER, S., and BACK, K., *Social Pressures in Informal Groups*, Harper and Brothers, New York, 1950.

6. FESTINGER, L., and THIBAUT, J., Interpersonal communications in small groups, *J. abnorm. soc. Psychol.*, 1951, 46, 92-100.

7. FESTINGER, L., GERARD, H., *et al.*, The influence process in the presence of extreme deviates, *Human Relations*, 1952, 5, 327-346.

8. FESTINGER, L., TORREY, J., and WILLERMAN, B., Self-evaluation as a function of attraction to the group, *Human Relations*, 1954.

9. GERARD, H., The effect of different dimensions of disagreement on the communication process in small groups, *Human Relations*, 1953, 6, 249-272.

10. HOFFMAN, P. J., FESTINGER, L., and LAWRENCE, D. H., Tendencies toward comparability in competitive bargaining, in *Human Relations*, 1954.

11. SCHACHTER, S., Deviation, rejection and communication, *J. abnorm. soc. Psychol.*, 1951, 46, 190-208.

8

The Role of the Psychological Situation in Determining the Direction of Human Behavior

JULIAN B. ROTTER
The Ohio State University

If a man were sitting alone in a library reading a book and an extremely pretty girl walked into the room, he would be likely to make an implicit or explicit sexual response. If he were at a Big Ten football game, in the course of an afternoon he might be expected to make several responses urging someone to murder either the officials or one or more players. If he were sitting in a classroom and one were to give him a test, he would strive for academic achievement. Now it is not news to anyone that the motivated or directional behavior of a human can be predicted to a large extent from the external environment, or what I shall call throughout the rest of this paper, the psychological situation. Nor is it a unique notion that unless the present cues are considered, prediction of behavior cannot be made regarding directionality, motivation or purposefulness of behavior. Theorists argue on what is the role or utility, if any, of a physiological conception of drive in predicting what might be called psychological or acquired behavior of human beings. However, it is my impression that they all agree that the specific directionality of the behavior, or any attempt to predict precisely or specifically what the human organism will do, requires a knowledge of the cues present, internal or external, and the acquired mean-

Reprinted from *The Nebraska Symposium* edited by Marshall R. Jones, University of Nebraska Press, 1955, with permission of the author and publishers.

ing or learned values that these cues have for the organism.

It is not my purpose in this paper to discuss the issue of the potential utility of a biological conception of drive in a systematic psychology. Although this is an important controversial issue, there has already been much attention devoted towards this problem. On the other hand, very little has been done to systematically include the complex psychological situation in prediction of human behavior. Indeed, after an exhaustive search of the literature for *systematic schema* to be used in predicting human behavior from specific situations, I am convinced that psychological climate is like weather, everyone talks about it but no one does anything about it.

Probably much of this neglect is due to the fact that theoretical psychologists, with the exception of those operating in the field of personality and social psychology, have not been greatly concerned with predicting specific behavior of mature human beings in complex situations. Where they have been concerned, they have noted the importance of the psychological situation, but little else. It is surprising in light of the actual data of behavior that so many personality theorists using faculties, traits, instincts, needs, habits, et cetera, have developed systems which purport to predict an individual's behavior all on the basis of some internal characteristic with little or no attention to the external conditions affecting the individual. Lewin (14), an exception to this approach, has dealt with the situation primarily in a formal manner but we can not tell from Lewin's approach whether the response of a person placed in a given psychological situation is going to be one directed at getting the recognition or love of other social objects present or is going to be directed at destroying them, until after the organism has acted. Cattell (6) has noted the importance of the situation in determining directional behavior and suggests some factor analysis of situations comparable to a factor analysis of traits. Coutu (7), a sociologist, speaks of the unit of behavior as a "tinsit" in which every unit is a combination of a tendency to behave brought to the situation by an organism and a situation itself. But Coutu furnishes no clues, methods, or data from which we can systematically build a formula for prediction.

One can multiply examples of why it is necessary to consider specific external conditions as well as stable personality characteristics in the prediction of behavior. Everyone is familiar with anecdotes of the submissive worker who is a tyrant at home, or the tyrant at work who is a timid soul around his wife. The so-called dependent personality may easily be observed on many specific occasions striving for recognition or status, and the individual who is characterized as domineering, status-oriented, etc., is frequently observed on social occasions as friendly, outgoing, helpful, and seeking the affection and regard of others.

However, anecdotal evidence is not all that is available to show the importance or the influence of the specific situation on behavior. Numerous studies on set, differences in instructions, and indeed the many experimental attempts to show generality of behavior, all support strongly the tremendous influence of the immediate situation on behavior. Not only does generality fail to appear in many studies, a fact which is frequently explained by uncontrolled aspects of the experimental situation, but when generality does appear, it is usually at a very low predictive level with a great share of the variance in behavior still unaccounted for. Now this is indeed a curious thing. In the half a century or more that psychologists have been interested in predicting the behavior of human beings in complex social situations they have persistently avoided the incontrovertible importance of the specific situation on behavior. They have assumed that if they could only produce a somewhat better schema for attempting to describe an individual's personality from a purely internal point of view they could somehow or other overcome this failure to predict. So they have gone from faculties and instincts and sentiments to traits, drives, needs, and the interaction of these within the individual, producing schema for personality organization and classification of internal states, but ignoring an analysis of the psychological situations in which human beings behave.

The practical implications of developing a method of describing and therefore being able to generalize about situations are considerable, and I might here only illustrate a few of these. From the point of view of a clinical psychologist, for example, if one were able to anticipate the characteristic behavior of an individual in given kinds of situations, this might help considerably in interpreting the significance of test results. Different individuals in the same situation and the same individual in different situations will react to cues by behavior directed towards different goals. Frequently these goals are quite at variance from those which the tester assumes to be present. Similarly, such knowledge would allow the clinician to anticipate the kinds of reactions a patient might have to different therapists and to different methods of therapy.

The problem of development of criteria for test validity could be analyzed not merely on the notion that the test is sampling some general characteristic which is likely to appear in any other place and time but rather that the test itself, the instructions, the place and the examiner are all part of a psychological situation and that what it measures most accurately is behavior in other situations of a similar kind. It is because of the erroneous assumption that the test should predict behavior regardless of the situation that validities tend to be so low. If we knew where to look for our validity, that is, in what situations to make a criterion measure, it is quite possible that we could find our psychological tests of considerably greater value. As a matter of fact, this would be true of all research in which an attempt is made to assess some characteristic of the individual for prediction of his behavior in something other than the test situation. For example, it has been found in the Air Force that a test for radar mechanics with high face validity has been nonpredictive of the behavior of these individuals on the job. This has been quite baffling to many. However, if the test situation is conceived of as being quite dissimilar to the job situation for which the predictions are made, such results are readily understood. It is conceivable that a test could be constructed and administered in such a way as to duplicate the motivational conditions of the job situation and would be able to measure what it set out to measure.

It is also true in many research studies that bewildering inconsistencies occur. For example, in the study of a relationship of ethnocentric attitudes and rigidity in problem solving, significant results of a directly opposite nature have been found in different studies (3, 12, 22). It seems likely that aspects of the testing situations apparently related to the personality of the examiner could account for these otherwise mysterious differences. The examiners presented cues which led to behavior directed towards different reinforcements in what would appear to be similar experimental situations. Analysis, therefore, of what are the significant variables in the psychological situation will lead to better research and to the opportunity for true replications. For a social psychologist such an analysis is absolutely necessary if he is actually to predict difference in the behavior of groups under varying conditions.

I am not intending to take a specifist position on personality but only to say that there are two basic aspects to the prediction of learned behavior. One deals with the individual's past experience, from which we must abstract constructs or variables of different levels of generality for different purposes and we attribute these to the individual or consider that he carries these around with him. The other is the present, meaningful environment, psychological situation, or what Lewin has called the "life space." From this latter variable the psychologists must also abstract constructs at different levels of generality for different purposes in order to predict behavior. The purpose of this paper is to discuss the latter aspect of prediction. It is not intended to imply that the manner in which abstractions are made about past experiences or the utility of biological, genetic or neurological variables in understanding the effects of experience are not also important problems.

I should like, therefore, before describing a social learning theory approach to this problem to review briefly some of the literature concerned with this problem of systematically utilizing the psychological situation in predicting the directional or motivated behavior of human beings.

In reviewing previous discussions of the effect of the psychological situation on motivated behavior, comments of some of the previous participants of the Nebraska Symposium on Motivation provide a general picture of how this concept has been treated in various current theories. Brown (2), has noted that internal and external cues or stimuli provide direction to a response. A concept of drive is not necessary to determine the specific direction of a response but rather provides for him an explanation of the energizing of behavior and of a concept of reinforcement. Harlow (11) has indicated that external stimulation is at least as important a source of behavior elicitation as internal stimulation. And Postman (19) finds both drive reduction and energizing as expendable concepts which leaves the prediction of behavior a function of learned stimulus-response relationships. He goes on to speak of the "projective fallacy," that is, that variations in perception are necessarily determined by internal motivational factors, and mentions the influence of set which is tied up with the situational context. Atkinson (1) and McClelland (15) likewise stress the importance of cues in determining behavior and Atkinson describes a simple method used by Jacobs for determining the normative potential of pictures for arousing particular classes of response dispositions. In describing the effect of cues, they make use of an expectancy construct.

Motivational psychologists concerned with the concept of drives, usually conceived of in physiological terms, such as hunger, thirst, or sex, have similarly directed attention to the importance of cues in determining the actual nature or direction of the organism's response. Animal psychologists have noted that, regardless of cyclical conditions of deprivation, food or water-seeking behavior occurs only in the presence of cues previously associated with food or water. Ford and Beach (9) have discussed in detail not only how sexual responses occur as a result of cues but they have also noted that as one goes up the phylogenetic scale the more important cues tend to be external rather than internal. Perhaps some distinction is needed here between internal versus external cues. By internal cues I mean that the individual is responding to stimuli conditions, arising in the body, with learned associative meanings, such as to a parched throat, or a pain in the region of the stomach. By external cues I refer to any aspect of the individual's environment, outside of the body, to which he is responding at any given time, and which for him has acquired meanings as a result of previous experience. A cue then is a psychological stimulus. One may learn to react in a given way to rumblings in the gastrointestinal tract just as one may learn to react in a given way to the presence of a member of the opposite sex. In short, then, motivational psychologists have universally agreed on the importance of stimuli or cues for determining behavior as, of course, have all learning psychologists. However, they have provided no schema for classifying such cues except for some of the internal cues which have been classified in terms of the presumed locus of the stimulation, for example, in the muscles of the throat, in the stomach, or in the sex organs.

Personality theorists have gone somewhat beyond this point in attempting some implicit or explicit method of classifying a psychological situation. At a practical level there has been a great deal of recent research on situational factors in psychological testing. Sarason (25) has published an excellent article analyzing some of the situational variables involved in intelligence testing, including such variables as the examiner, the purpose of the test, the instructions, the set of the examinee. Recent research on projective tests has resulted in at least suggestive evidence that different types of results may be expected as a function of the sex and personality of the examiner and the physical place of testing (10, 13). When such attempts can be put on a predictive basis, then one may speak of a crude classification of psychological situations leading to predictions of different kinds of behavior.

In other clinical writing there have been implicit suggestions for taking into account the psychological situations in various personality theories. In psychoanalysis, for example, two variables are frequently mentioned; one is the sex of the social object present, the other is whether the social object present is a peer or an authority figure, that is, a father, mother or parent surrogate. Thus, it is possible not merely to say that an individual is anxious, but that he is or is not anxious in peer or authority situations or that he is or is not anxious in heterosexual situations or homosexual situations or any combination of these two variables. It should be pointed out, however, that these distinctions and how they are made are not systematically described but are implicit in the writings of Freud and other psychoanalysts. Various clinical and perceptual approaches also have used, by implication, a crude division of situations into threatening versus non-threatening, anxiety-provoking versus nonanxiety-provoking, or stressful versus nonstressful (20).

Perhaps the most extensive suggestion for actually classifying psychological situations comes from Murray (16). Murray has suggested that situations are susceptible of classification in terms of the different kinds of effects they exert on the subject. Such effects he refers to as *press* and divides them into two kinds, "benefits" and "harms." Although Murray has not made an exhaustive schema for analyzing such press, he describes them in terms of their effects on the needs of the individual and states that situations should be classified in terms of their interaction with the person's needs. Thus, for each of his needs, one may speak of a situation which is potentially satisfying or frustrating to that need. For example, there could be gratifying dependency situations and frustrating dependency situations, gratifying harm-avoidance situations and frustrating harm-avoidance situations, et cetera. As to specific methods of determining what needs one should utilize or how to go about identifying situations for predictive purposes, Murray provides no systematic suggestions.

Psychologists interested in the psychology of perception have oriented some research around a somewhat different variable for describing psychological situations as they may affect behavior, by classification of situations into structured and unstructured (4). Individuals with different personality characteristics or social attitudes might be expected to react differentially in these two kinds of situations. The systematic definition of structured and unstructured, however, has not always been made clear.

Brunswik (5) has repeatedly emphasized what he considers to be the important but neglected task of sampling psychological situations in order to predict behavior, which method he contrasts with the more characteristic approach to prediction by sampling individuals. Brunswik does not provide a schema but does suggest that psychological situations or specific cues to situations should be analyzed in terms of their probability or expectancy values for the individual.

A third group of social scientists concerned with the problem of predicting behavior from the psychological situation has been the sociologists and social psychologists. Possibly Thomas (28), from the point of view of a sociologist, has stressed this most heavily. The concept of situational determination is basic to the general notion that the behavior of organisms depends upon social roles and the assumption that the behavior is characteristic of the particular role one has or the expectancies that others have of one. Newcomb (17) has perhaps described this position most systematically, emphasizing the importance of expectations of consequences in determining role behavior. The social psychologists concerned with attitudes have implicitly suggested various schema for classifying situations on the basis of social objects so they imply that one may anticipate a certain kind of behavior from social objects who are identified as Negroes, Jews, foreigners, et cetera. However, there is still to be noted an absence of any explicit approach to the problem of classification of actual life situations.

In summary then, a few schema, mostly implicit, have been suggested for dealing with psychological situations. These have been related for the most part to specific empirical problems. Thus, there are some limited classifications of testing situations, interpersonal situations from the point of view of adjustment, interpersonal situations from the point of view of social attitudes, and interpersonal situations from the point of view of role expectations. It might seem at this time that I am preparing to burst forth with a pat schema of my own. Unfortunately, this is not the case, but I would like to suggest some ways which an experimental attack may be made on the problem from a social learning point of view. This point of view has been recently described in some detail (23), but I should like here to briefly recapitulate only some of the basic assumptions related to the present topic.

This Social Learning Theory may be described as a

molar behavior theory employing an empirical law of effect. It uses both an expectancy construct and a reinforcement construct but does not utilize any concept of drive reduction. The basic formula for behavior employs three constructs. The first of these is *behavior potential,* which is the potentiality of any behavior occurring in any given situation or situations as calculated in relation to any single reinforcement or set of reinforcements. *Expectancy,* the second, is defined as the probability held by the individual that a particular reinforcement will occur as a function of a specific behavior on his part in a specific situation or situations. Expectancy is independent of the value or importance of the reinforcement. *Reinforcement value,* the third basic construct, is defined as the degree of preference for any reinforcement to occur if the possibilities of occurrence of this and other reinforcements are equal. These constructs are related as shown in the formula below.

1. $B.P._{x, s_1, R_a} = f(E_{x, R_a, s_1} \& R.V._{a_1, s_1})$

This formula may be read as follows: The potential for behavior x to occur in situation 1 in relation to reinforcement a is a function of the expectancy of the occurrence of reinforcement a following behavior x in situation 1, and the value of reinforcement a in situation 1.

It can be noted in this formula that the psychological situation or s plays a role in the determination of all basic measures. However, the specific way in which the measures are involved is through the influence of the situation on the expectancies of the individual. What the situation provides is cues which are related through previous experience to expectancies for behavior-reinforcement sequences. Perhaps stated more simply, what the situation provides is cues which tell the individual what behaviors he may expect will be followed by what reinforcements. Such expectancies are, of course, quantifiable on a scale from zero to one hundred. The potentiality of any behavior occurring in any situation, then, since it is determined by expectancy, is in turn determined by the situation. In order to see how a situation affects the value or preference value of a reinforcement, we need to examine the formula for the value of a reinforcement. This is given below.

$$2.\ \mathrm{R.V.}_{\cdot a,\ s_1} = f(\mathrm{E}_{\mathrm{R}_a \to \mathrm{R}_{(b\text{-}n)},\ s_1} \ \& \ \mathrm{R.V.}_{\cdot (b\text{-}n),\ s_1})$$

This formula may be read as follows: The value of reinforcement a in situation 1 is a function of the expectancies that this reinforcement will lead to the subsequent reinforcements b to n in situation 1, and the values of these subsequent reinforcements b to n in situation 1. In other words, reinforcements do not occur entirely independently of one another and the occurrence of one reinforcement may have expected consequences for future reinforcements. This expectancy is referred to as E_2 and it too may be tied to a particular situation. For example, depending on the nature of the audience and the nature of the compliment, a personal compliment may result in one situation in a feeling of satisfaction and in another situation, in a feeling of embarrassment. However, in general, the values of reinforcements are more stable from situation to situation than are expectancies that particular reinforcements will follow specific behaviors. This seems logical since subsequent reinforcements are frequently delayed and are not likely to be a part of the situation in which the original reinforcement occurred.

A study by Schroder and Rotter (26) illustrates how situational cues affect expectancy for behavior reinforcement sequences. In this study different groups of subjects were trained in a simple problem-solving situation to have increasing degrees of expectation for reinforcement for looking for new alternatives. The cues of the training situation elicited behavior of looking for alternatives, in a changed experimental situation, in the four different groups in the same order as the expectancies generated in training. There is nothing about this study which uniquely shows the relation between cues and expectancy for behavior-reinforcement sequences. Any study of learning can be analyzed in a similar fashion.

A study by Phares (18) provides a clear illustration of how reinforcement values are likewise affected by situational cues although they also show considerable stability from situation to situation. Phares had grade school, male students rank prejudged and equated reinforcements which were classified as academic recognition, athletic recognition and manual skill recognition in three different settings. The rankings were made by different students in the woodworking shop, gymnasium, and English class. He obtained differences along predicted lines indicating the influence of the situational cues on reinforcement value.

It is necessary to discuss the concept of *need potential* before going on to suggestions for categorizing life situations. In social learning theory, a need is considered not as an internal drive or push but as a potential to respond with any one of a set of functionally related behaviors directed towards one or more of a functionally related set of reinforcements. The strength of a need for recognition, for example, is directly measured by the frequency with which the individual exhibits behaviors in any set of situations which are oriented towards changing the environment to increase the potential occurrence of recognition reinforcements as compared to other kinds of reinforcements.

The use of the term *functionally related* here has an empirical reference. Two behaviors or two reinforcements are functionally related if one changes as a result of a change in the strength of another. The greater the change in the second through a process of generalization, the greater is the nature of the functional relationship. Another empirical basis for functional relationships is that of substitutability under certain conditions where one behavior is blocked or a reinforcement does not occur. By experimental study it is possible to develop need concepts or concepts based on the directionality of behavior which are of predictive value for any given culture. When the concepts are empirically arrived at for an individual through clinical study then they will have predictive value for that individual. In this way an empirical and logical basis is provided for considering a person's behavior in terms of broader generalized categories (i.e., he is a highly dependent person) without necessitating a trait, faculty, typological, or instinctual approach to personality. Such descriptions, however, must be limited by some reference to the situations in which the behavior is presumed to occur and the organization of behavior reinforcement sequences into psychological needs must be described as characteristic only of the particular culture in which the classification is made. Behaviors that bring love, approval, disapproval, praise, and so on in one culture will differ considerably from those which bring the same reinforcements in another culture.

Although it is true that a functional similarity will appear between behaviors or reinforcements, the amount of such similarity is determined by the degree to which these events have led to the same or similar reinforcements in the experience of the particular subject. Consequently, one might expect that the more any classification scheme is broadened, the less functional similarity will exist between any two randomly selected behaviors or reinforcements included in that classification. Stated another way, intercorrelations of reinforcement values or of behavior potentials within any need will tend to be lower as the classification is more broadly conceived and made more inclusive. The more limited and specific the classification, the higher the functional similarity of any two randomly selected behaviors within the need, and the higher the predictability from one behavior potential or reinforcement value to another within the same classification. These inferences appear to be supported by Rockwell's (21) and Dean's (8) study of the generality of needs.

In Rockwell's study a large number of different referents for strength of need were intercorrelated for six broad need areas. Recognition and status, dominance independence, protection-dependency, love and affection and physical comfort were the needs investigated. Her results suggested that higher intercorrelations appeared within the less inclusive categories. Dean's investigation dealt more specifically with the problem. Dean attempted to predict behavior on a level of aspiration task from estimates of generalized expectancy made from increasingly more general categories or need concepts. The least inclusive was made from a measure of expectancy for success on a similar task. More inclusive were estimates based on interviews to determine the general level of expectancy for success in the area of motor coordination as a whole. Most inclusive was an estimate, from separate interviews, for expectancy for success in general for all kinds of behavior excluding motor coordination tasks. He found correlations in the predicted direction. The least inclusive category predicted expectancies at the highest level (Pearsonian r .70). The middle category estimate correlated next most highly (Eta .42) and the most inclusive category estimate correlated the lowest (Eta .26). All correlations were significant.

Perhaps at this point a more systematic definition of what has been referred to as the psychological situation or sometimes *cue* or *stimulus* is called for. Like Lewin and the Gestalt psychologists social learning theory would assume that a person reacts to the totality of his psychological environment. However, he also reacts to specific aspects of it, and within a given situation the presence of different cues may set up conflicts or expectancies for quite different outcomes for the same behavior. As psychologists, we may be interested in his reaction to the situation as a whole, and we may also be interested in analyzing this down to its specific cues. How we describe a specific situation must be determined by our immediate purpose and the degree of predictive efficiency we are willing to sacrifice for reasons of time economy. If for a given purpose it is sufficient to fasten upon some specific cue or stimulus object to make the necessary predictions, other aspects of the situation may well be neglected. If it is found empirically that other aspects of the situation when considered result in significantly higher prediction, then description of the psychological situation must be extended to include these cues as well.

It would seem useful here to make a distinction between identifying a situation for purposes of communication and categorizing or classifying a situation psychologically. The basic principle for classifying or categorizing a situation is psychological, that is, subjective, in that situations are categorized in terms of the meanings which they have for an individual or a group and measured by some kind of verbal or nonverbal response. However, it is not necessary to fall into a "phenomenological" error. Situations can be *identified* on the basis of objective characteristics, that is, by descriptions at the sensory level which result in high agreement among subjects and judges. Although we may categorize a classroom, a football game, a superior officer, a church, or a therapist psychologically, according to the acquired meaning these have for subjects or according to the expectancies that subjects have built up about them, we nevertheless identify what it is that we are talking about in nonsystematic, common-sense language which if necessary can be easily translated into sensory level descriptions. In this way there is no question of communication about what it is that is being referred to.

It might be said here, parenthetically, that the same thing would be true in this theory when referring to behaviors or reinforcements. Because a system is psychological and its variables as systematically conceived deal with acquired meanings is no reason why the system may be thought of or should be thought of as lacking in objectivity. Behaviors, reinforcements, and situations may be identified in objective terms although their significance and systematic formulae are concerned with constructs relating to personal or acquired meanings.

Although the concepts presented have been most sketchy, the above discussion is intended to provide some background for the suggestion that situations be categorized or classified in any given culture in a similar fashion to need potential. That is, they are categorized on the basis of experimentally determined similarities related to the nature of the reinforcements that are likely to occur. Two situations are similar if in a given culture the probability of particular reinforcements occurring in those two situations as a result of specific behaviors are also similar. After determining situational similarity we can refer to academic recognition situations, love and affection situations, conformity situations, social acceptance situations, athletic skill situations, physical comfort situations or of situations which combine these possibilities in any particular way. As in the case of categorizing needs, one might think of situations being categorized one way for a culture or group but differently for individuals. It would not be assumed that the way in which a situation is most frequently categorized in a given culture is the way in which every person in the culture categorized it, and clinical psychologists interested in individual prediction would be primarily concerned with the differences between individual and cultural categorization. In fact, such differences should be diagnostic or post-dictive of previous differences in training or experience. The cultural studies, however, should yield the terms or categories which provide the starting place for the analysis of individual differences.

As in the case of needs, there is no finite list of situations or situational categories which can be arrived at. The number and kind of situational distinctions one would make would be determined by (1) the purpose one has in classifying situations and (2) the level of prediction or accuracy of prediction required. The higher the prediction desired, the more distinctions need to be made or the more specific the situational categories used. For example, in trying to predict behavior if we spoke of love and affection situations, there would be less prediction about behavior from one situation to another than if we spoke of love from opposite sex peer situations as differentiated from love from same sex peers or love from parents.

I would like now to turn to the problem of determining situational similarity. Logical analysis suggests four methods that may be used. These all should produce similar or comparable results.

The first method may be described as that of sampling expectancies. If a group of subjects from a given culture are asked to estimate their expectations for the potential occurrence of given kinds of reinforcements in specific situations, it would then be possible to classify these situations as similar or dissimilar on the basis of such expectancies. Studies regarding the use of an expectancy construct in behavior-reinforcement sequences have made many methodological advances, and have suggested that fairly accurate statements of verbal responses can be obtained regarding such expectancies (24).

The second method would be to actually sample by an observational technique the actual reinforcements which occur in given situations. For example, in comparable time samples judges could record the number of times in the classroom that reinforcements for academic or intellectual skill occur in contrast to the number of times the same reinforcements occur on the playground. Such a method involves practical difficulties but not theoretical ones. For many specific purposes the method may be quite feasible.

A third method is that of actually sampling behaviors. Behaviors would already be classified in terms of the reinforcements they are usually directed towards, for example, aggressive behavior towards dominance, friendly behavior directed towards social acceptance and competitive or striving behavior towards recognition. Then situations which produce the same behaviors can be categorized as similar. Some attempts to carry out research of this kind are now in the planning stage at Ohio State. The subjects are given a large number of situations and then are asked to rate the probability of their using each of a long series of possible behaviors in each situation. Factor analysis would indicate what situations would tend to produce the same behaviors or the same pattern of behaviors. Of course this is a paper and pencil approach presenting some methodological problems; observational techniques for measuring behavior are also possible, although more difficult from a practical standpoint.

The final method to be suggested is that of measuring generalization. This may be studied either by reference to behaviors, expectancies, or reinforcement values. The paradigm here is to pre-test some behavior potential in several situations, then to increase or decrease this behavior potential in one situation and test in the other situations for a generalization of the increase or decrease. Similar tests of generalization can be made for changes in expectancy or reinforcement value. Where generalization is greater, situational similarity is greater. For example, the value of the reinforcement of adult praise for children could be assessed in the classroom, on the playground, and in Sunday School. This value may be reduced experimentally in the classroom and then tested for change on the playground and in Sunday School. A greater generalization of the reduction would be found in the situation most like the original. Similar techniques could be employed in a generalization of changes of behavior potential or expectancy.

A study of this type was done with rats by Schroder and Rotter (27). In this study one group of rats was trained to go in one direction in a white or black maze with rough or smooth floor for one reinforcement and to go in the other direction in a maze of opposite color and different floor for a different reinforcement (food and water). The second group was similarly trained except that the reinforcement in both mazes was the same (either food or water). A balanced design was employed to control maze cues, direction of turning and type of reinforcement, and control was exercised on amount of deprivation. Both groups were then extinguished in one maze and tested for generalization of extinction to the other. The hypothesis was strongly supported that generalization of extinction from one situation to the other was greater when the rewards in the two situations were the same than when they were different.

The methods described would result in classification of situations according to similarity in the kinds of reinforcements which typically occur in a given culture or subculture. When classifications are built up a logical basis should appear for anticipating behavior in situations not previously studied.

There are other ways of looking upon the problem of classification which may be fruitful for given purposes. Functional similarity in these classifications may still be tested with any of the four methods described above. While it is hypothesized in this theory that similarity of situations occurs as a result of similarity in past reinforcements, the situations themselves may be conveniently categorized by particular, outstanding cues. In this way one might think of people as situations. Classifications such as those based on sex differences, peer versus authority relationships or dominant versus subservient relationships may have particular utility for special problems. In any case, it is hypothesized that where functional equivalence occurs among situations, the degree of equivalence is related to the degree of similarity in the reinforcements which may be expected in the situations. The reinforcements themselves which would be regarded as similar, in order to test such a hypothesis, would first have to be determined empirically from clinical studies and group studies of individuals in the same culture.

Social psychologists may find utility in grouping people in other ways such as by race, religion, skin color, et cetera. It may also be valuable for some purposes to analyze situations in terms of such formal characteristics as the number of relevant cues present and degree of competition among cues. Situations may also be characterized for some purposes in terms of the height of the expectancies attached to the cues or combination of cues present. We refer to unstructured situations where expectations are low versus structured ones where expectations are high. Some research in social psychology has also utilized what I would refer to as ambiguous versus non-ambiguous situations. These would be ones where the cues are not easily identified, as compared to those where the cues are easily identified. Although it is not always necessary to identify or categorize the situations in terms of expected reinforcements, it seems to me that in most cases an analysis in these terms allows greater prediction. This is particularly true when one is seeking efficient methods of changing behavior or what some would call attitudes in these situations. I am suggesting that in social psychology the analysis of the expectancies for reinforcement for different kinds of social objects will enhance and increase the present body of knowledge regarding how changes in attitudes may be most efficiently effected.

SUMMARY

This paper has been concerned with the problem of the prediction of directional or motivated aspects of behavior from the psychological situation. I have tried to indicate the importance of the categorization or classification of situations for the general purpose of prediction of human behavior and also the comparative neglect of theorizing and research in this area. The paper has also attempted, perhaps too sketchily, to make an analysis of this problem from a social learning point of view.

It is hypothesized in this point of view that the situation functions mainly as a set of cues which are related to expectancies held by the individual for behavior-reinforcement sequences. Consequently, potential behaviors likely to occur in given situations may be predicted in part once it is known what kinds of reinforcements subjects from a given culture anticipate will occur in that situation. In short, situations may be characterized in a manner parallel to that in which needs are characterized within social learning theory. The method is not an *a priori* one based on presumed physiological or other inherent drives but an empirical one in which groupings are made on the basis of factual criteria.

Four methods for empirical investigation of similarity in situations have been suggested. These methods are yet to be tried and specific operations for implementing them are yet to be tested. However, the general methodologies have already been utilized with some success in studies where people rather than situations are the conditions which are varied.

It is unfortunate that theoretical analyses do not substitute for research. Before actual predictions can be made regarding the behavior of groups or individuals as a function of their psychological situation, it will be necessary to carry out exhaustive research for each culture group which is an object of study.

REFERENCES

1. ATKINSON, J. W. Explorations using imaginative thought to assess the strength of human motives. In *Nebraska Symposium on Motivation, 1954.* Marshall R. Jones (Ed.). Lincoln: Univ. of Nebraska Press, 1954.

2. BROWN, J. S. Problems presented by the concept of acquired drives. In *Current Theory and Research in Motivation.* Lincoln: Univ. of Nebraska Press, 1953.

3. BROWN, R. W. A determinant of the relationship between rigidity and authoritarianism. *J. abnorm. soc. Psychol.* 1953, 48, 469-476.

4. BRUNER, J. S. Perceptual theory and the Rorschach Test. *J. of Personal.* 1948, 17, 157-168.

5. Brunswik, E. Organismic achievement and environmental probability. *Psychol. Rev.*, 1943, 50, 255-272.

6. Cattell, R. B. *Personality. A Systematic Theoretical and Factual Study.* New York: McGraw-Hill, 1950.

7. Coutu, W. *Emergent Human Nature.* New York: Knopf, 1949.

8. Dean, S. J. Sources of variance in individual statements of expectancy. Unpublished doctor's dissertation. The Ohio State Univ., 1953.

9. Ford, C. S., and Beach, F. A. *Patterns of Sexual Behavior.* New York: Harper & Bros., 1952.

10. Gibby, R. G., Miller, N. R., and Walker, E. L. The examiner's influence on the Rorschach protocol. *J. consult. Psychol.*, 1953, 17, 425-428.

11. Harlow, H. F. Motivation as a factor in new responses. In *Current Theory and Research in Motivation.* Lincoln: Univ. of Nebraska Press, 1953.

12. Levitt, E. E., and Zelen, S. L. The validity of the Einstellung Test as a measure of rigidity. *J. abnorm. soc. Psychol.*, 1953, 48, 573-580.

13. Lord, E. E. Experimentally induced variations in Rorschach performance. *Psychol. Monogr.*, 1950, 65, No. 10, 1-34.

14. Lewin, K. *Principles of Topological Psychology.* New York: McGraw-Hill, 1936.

15. McClelland, D. The achievement motive in its social context. In *Nebraska Symposium on Motivation, 1955.* Marshall R. Jones (Ed.). Lincoln: Univ. of Nebraska Press, 1955.

16. Murray, H. Toward a classification of interaction. In *Toward a General Theory of Action.* T. Parsons and E. A. Shils (Eds.). Cambridge: Harvard Univ. Press, 1952.

17. Newcomb, T. *Social Psychology.* New York: Dryden Press, 1950.

18. Phares, J. Situational factors in the determination of reinforcement values. Unpublished master's thesis. The Ohio State Univ., 1953.

19. Postman, L. Comments on papers by Brown and Harlow. In *Current Theory and Research in Motivation.* Lincoln: Univ. of Nebraska Press, 1953.

20. Postman, L., and Bruner, J. S. Perception under stress. *Psychol. Rev.*, 1948, 55, 314-323.

21. Rockwell, A. F. The evaluation of six social learning need constructs. Unpublished doctor's dissertation. The Ohio State Univ., 1950.

22. Rokeach, M. Generalized mental rigidity as a factor in

ethnocentricism. *J. abnorm. soc. Psychol.*, 1948, 43, 259-278.

23. ROTTER, J. B. *Social Learning and Clinical Psychology.* New York: Prentice-Hall, 1954.

24. ROTTER, J. B., FITZGERALD, B. J., and JOYCE, J. A comparison of some objective measures of expectancy. *J. abnorm. soc. Psychol.*, 1954, 49, 111-114.

25. SARASON, S. The test situation and the problem of prediction. *J. clin. Psychol.*, 1950, 6, 387-392.

26. SCHRODER, H. M., and ROTTER, J. B. Rigidity as learned behavior. *J. exp. Psychol.*, 1952, 44, 141-150.

27. SCHRODER, H. M., and ROTTER, J. B. Generalization of expectancy changes as a function of the nature of reinforcement. *J. exp. Psychol.*, 1954, 48, 343-348.

28. THOMAS, W. I. *Social Behavior and Personality.* New York: Social Science Research Council, 1951.

Index